Have You Ever Wondered?

The Origins of Our Colloquial Heritage

by

Smith Ely Goldsmith

To Earl with best wishes from Ely

DORRANCE PUBLISHING CO., INC.
PITTSBURGH, PENNSYLVANIA 15222

W9-CJT-658

ISBN # 0-8059-4274-2
Printed in the United States of America

Second Printing

For information or to order additional books, please write:
Dorrance Publishing Co., Inc.
643 Smithfield Street
Pittsburgh, Pennsylvania 15222
U.S.A.

Dedicated to:

My wife, Ann, and brother, Dolf, who, along with many friends and other family members, have contributed their editing skills, colloquial knowledge and moral support, without which this project would not have been possible.

Cover created by
Christiann B. Goldsmith

Contents

Acknowledgments

The author gratefully acknowledges the kind and valuable assistance of the following:

McWilliam & Lucy Bollman	New York, NY
Bill & Ann Butler	Glens Falls, NY
Pamela Clarke	Glens Falls, NY
Joseph Cribb	Canandaigua, NY
Byron & Caroline Delavan	Canandaigua, NY
Jay & Barbara Erlichman	New York, NY
Ann Louise Goldsmith	New York, NY
Christiann B. Goldsmith	Santa Barbara, CA
Dolf & Alice Goldsmith	San Antonio, TX
Helena A. Goldsmith	San Franciso, CA
Louise W. Grogan	Plano, TX
Tim & Lila Healy	New York, NY
Fred & Alice Irving	Jacksonville, FL
John Kantner	Santa Barbara, CA
Edwin F. Libby	Manchester, ME
Jim & Thelma Mrazek	Bethesda, MD
Priscilla Snyder	New York, NY
John Michael White	Gulf Stream, FL
Lucy White	New York, NY
Robin & Jane Zee	Baltimore, MD

Foreword

In December of 1939 our family left the Netherlands and settled in New York City, introducing me to a strange new language called English. Along with various grammatical and spelling peculiarities I soon discovered the existence of numerous rich but incomprehensible expressions. Just imagine my confusion when told at the tender age of nine that, as a newcomer I had, **a hard row to hoe**, my room must be kept in **apple pie order**, and success resulting from hard work was **a lead pipe cinch**.

Family and friends soon realized my need to learn, as well as my fascination with, these wonderful phrases. With their help I eventually absorbed a fair amount of collective knowledge relating to the origins of colloquialisms, quotations, and individual words. The purpose of this book is an attempt to document a number of the more interesting examples. With this idea in mind, I have combined my own recollections with historical perspectives and miscellaneous information gleaned from a variety of sources.

In spite of my efforts some of these anecdotes may still be considered controversial or even inaccurate. Because of this possibility reader's comments, additional information or different points of view, will be more than welcome.

Just in the Nick of Time
Pigeonholed
Red Tape
Sweep Under the Rug
Called on the Carpet
Reading the Riot Act

For centuries the government of Great Britain relied on a unique bookkeeping system. Loans made to the Crown were recorded in a normal fashion, but repayments were noted by cutting a notch in a wooden stick or "talley." Tallies were also "nicked" to keep track of points earned during sporting events, allowing unexpected victories from last minute scores to arrive **just in the nick of time**. Even though England abandoned her archaic record keeping system in 1826, we have perpetuated the practice of proclaiming **just in the nick of time** for honoring a variety of last minute accomplishments.

Discarded tallies were chopped up for firewood without engendering any great sense of loss. English bureaucrats were not so easily parted from their large roll top desks containing numerous small compartments resembling pigeon houses. Documents possessing embarrassing potential were frequently **pigeonholed**, meaning they somehow gravitated to the most inaccessible of these dark crevasses, never to see the light of day again.

Non-sensitive papers moved smoothly along the civil service path in the form of bundles tied together with long red ribbons, so that **red tape** came to symbolize the machinations of Great Britain's government. Years later, Washington Irving was credited for popularizing the concept of **red tape** in our country by describing politicians as having "brains little better than red tape and parchment." Further comment would be superfluous, since few of us reach our allotted life span without participating in numerous bureaucratic **red tape** confrontations.

Nineteenth century French officials favored ornately carpeted offices, and subordinates accused of **pigeonholing** or **sweeping issues** (as opposed to dirt) **under the rug**, were frequently **called on the carpet** and **read the riot act**. Reading the riot act stems from the rule of George I, England's most unpopular Hanoverian monarch. His imperial attitude, coupled with a refusal to learn the English language, sparked a series of violent protests. In 1714 Parliament responded to this wave of civil disobedience with passage of the Riot Act. Unruly gatherings were now **read the Riot Act**, an ornately worded proclamation with a bottom line message: disperse or go to jail.

The Whole Nine Yards
Rule of Thumb

Initial research indicated that **the whole nine yards** came from the nine cubic yard capacity of a modern day cement mixer. Translating this nugget of information into an interesting anecdote would have presented a severe challenge. Luckily for author and reader alike, further study has unearthed a much more fascinating origin for this commonly used colloquialism.

Relatively few Americans recognize the name of Hiram Stevens Maxim (1840-1916), who was actually one of our country's greatest inventors. This self taught genius not only preceded Edison in creating an incandescent lamp but also designed a flyable steam powered airplane thirteen years before the Wright brothers' famous flight. Even though poor patent protection cost Maxim dearly in the lighting endeavor, his prolific contributions to the science of electricity panicked his competitors. Eventually they offered, and he accepted, the then huge sum of $20,000 per year for ten years to leave the electrical field.

Unlike Edison and other inventors, Maxim had often been unable to translate his ideas into money-making consumer products. Maxim moved to Europe where his fortunes changed for the better after securing financial backing for his long-nurtured notion that a rapid fire, portable "machine gun" was possible. Capitalizing on a very simple idea, he used the explosive force generated by the firing of one cartridge to load the next one. Maxim's ability to envision a clear solution for a complex problem, coupled with the development of smokeless powder and higher quality cartridges, now combined to create a most fearsome weapon of war.

The development of the airplane proceeded on a parallel course with improved variations of Maxim's machine gun, and World War I provided a catalyst hastening the inevitable marriage of these two new inventions. Although little standardization existed, machine gun belts made of metal links held approximately four hundred rounds and were about nine yards long. Upon completion of their day's activities, pilots often answered queries relating to ammunition expenditure with, "I shot off **the whole nine yards**" meaning, of course, all of it. Ground troops and occupants of other flying machines quickly learned the art of camouflage and evasive tactics lest they find themselves subjected to a hail of enemy gunfire. The machine guns of those days soon became obsolete, but we remain firmly wedded to the concept of acquiring or receiving **the whole nine yards'** worth of information, as opposed to bullets.

Standard source material indicates that **rule of thumb** originated with an old time practice whereby brewmasters used their thumbs for testing each brew's temperature. As in the case of **the whole nine yards**, additional research has revealed the existence of a much more interesting **rule of thumb** background.

Wife-beating in Medieval England was not considered worthy of restraint. The law did, however, provide the fairer sex with one small measure of protection, in that instruments of torture could not exceed the thickness of a husband's thumb. Savvy maidens contemplating marriage thus availed themselves of the **rule of thumb** by choosing partners endowed with skinny digits.

According to Hoyle
Bridge
Left in the Lurch
Back to Square One
Back to the Drawing Board

Edmond Hoyle lived from 1672 to 1769, an amazing feat of endurance for those days. His working life was spent as a minor bureaucrat in the Irish government, and only upon retirement did Hoyle immortalize his name by recognizing and filling a most pressing need.

Playing cards had been in existence for hundreds of years before Hoyle's time. Many similar card games or variations of the same game existed, each of which sported its own set of complex rules. Not surprisingly, this state of affairs created an atmosphere of continuous irritation and confusion. Starting with whist, a forerunner of bridge, Hoyle codified and published a set of rules covering the games of his time. This achievement enhanced Hoyle's reputation so thoroughly that his name became equated with correct social behavior, causing us to exclaim it's **according to Hoyle**, once we are satisfied that proper protocol has been observed.

In 1878 a number of British military advisors to the Turkish government happened to be quartered in Istanbul. With time on their hands and a copy of Hoyle's book, they invented a new card game based on whist. Since their billet was on the other side of the Golden Horn from the coffee houses where the game's converts habitually gathered, daily pilgrimages over a connecting bridge were required. Their less active colleagues coined the word **bridge** for this new pastime, which eventually reached London where it was refined and exported round the globe.

Board games have been in existence much longer than playing cards. The ancient Greeks favored a board and dice game that was later popularized in France as lourche and eventually passed on to us as backgammon. Lourche rules specified that if one player finished while his opponent's moves were less than half completed, the latter was in a "lurch." Cribbage contains a similar lurch rule applicable to losers with a board count below 31 out of a possible 61. Losing these games by more than a "lurch" margin, or dealing with disappointments engendered by poor performance on the part of those we trust, thus tends to leave us with the sinking feeling of having been **left in the lurch**.

Both chess and checker boards contain sixty-four squares, one of which is referred to as square one. Little imagination is required to explain why starting projects anew brings us **back to square one**. If this seems somewhat trite, we may do marginally better by substituting **back to the drawing board**. The latter has nothing to do with games of chance or skill and probably originated with Peter Arno's well known cartoon depicting an airplane designer walking away from the wreckage of his latest effort.

The Devil's Advocate
Let the Devil Take the Hindmost
Let the Chips Fall Where They May
That's How the Cookie Crumbles
That's the Way the Ball Bounces

Contrary to popular supposition the word *"devil"* did not come from "do-evil." When the Old Testament was translated into Greek, the Hebrew word *"Satan,"* which meant "adversary," became *"diabolos"* or "accuser." In Middle English, diabolos was changed to *"deofol,"* the pronunciation of which led us to "devil."

Throughout its early history, the Roman Catholic Church played a key role as both guardian and dispenser of mankind's substantial, but nonetheless incomplete, trove of accumulated knowledge. Legends and superstitions, many of which alluded to the devil, were thus easy to sell and served to fill out gaps in the church's collective store of information.

Candidates for sainthood were represented by a proponent or *"advocatus dei"* (God's advocate) and opposed by an *"advocatus diaboli"* (devil's advocate). The latter produced every conceivable negative argument, splitting hairs to the point where we have appropriated the role of **the devil's advocate** for making mountains out of molehills.

One superstition of unknown origin involving the devil was popularized in an Elizabethan play called *Philaster* and concerned a school run by the devil in Toledo, Spain. Candidates for graduation were required to run through underground passages with the devil in hot pursuit. The slowest, or hindmost, student was invariably captured by the devil and became his personal slave. The sequel to this unlikely legend was that **let the devil take the hindmost** came to represent the certainty that none of us ever completely control our own destiny.

Future generations changed the description of this unpleasant reality to **let the chips fall where they may**. Unfortunately, the dumbing down of our language continues unabated, and **letting the chips fall where they may** has given way to **that's the way the cookie crumbles** and the even more juvenile **that's the way the ball bounces**.

Cold War
Pyrrhic Victory
Iron Curtain
Bamboo Curtain

In 281 B.C. a military alliance was forged between the Greek city of Tarentium, located 250 miles south of Rome, and the Kingdom of Epirus, occupying the approximate area of today's Albania. Shortly thereafter Tarentium foolishly challenged the power of a rapidly expanding Rome, forcing King Pyrrhus of Epirus to honor his mutual defense commitment. His prompt arrival with twenty-five thousand troops not only constituted a remarkable logistic achievement but also precipitated the first recorded conflict between Greek and Roman cultures at a place called Heraclea.

Greek forces won the day and, after several years of inconclusive maneuvering, managed a repeat performance at Asculum. Rome did not feel threatened by these backwoods clashes and thus refused all offers of reconciliation as long as foreign troops maintained a physical presence within her sphere of influence.

Beset by frustration over a stalemate that eroded his army's strength and sapped his men's fighting spirit, Pyrrhus proposed marching on Rome herself. Unfortunately, the very mention of such an ambitious project caused Pyrrhus' Greek allies to silently fade away, forcing him to exercise his only remaining option. The King of Epirus sailed for home with the remnants of his army, tallied up the score, and sadly concluded he could ill afford any more victories of this nature.

Since the days of King Pyrrhus there have been numerous instances of conflicts resolved at unacceptable costs. The United States, for example, won the **cold war** (from Walter Lippman's 1947 book on U.S.-Soviet relations titled *"The Cold War"*) by spending rather than fighting the Soviet Union into oblivion. Keeping in mind King Pyrrhus' astute observation, we may someday find that replacing the Russian "bear" with a collection of fragmented, unstable states will have earned America a **pyrrhic victory** as well.

In early 1945, Nazi Germany resembled a rotten melon about to be crushed in a giant vise comprised of American-led forces and the Soviet Union. Fearing future conflicts among the superpowers over the control of post-war Europe, the United States, Great

Britain, and the Soviet Union conferred at Yalta for the purpose of dividing the continent into zones of occupation. Unfortunately, no amount of good will could placate the fear and paranoia resulting from Europe's partition, providing fertile ground for a fifty year long **cold war.**

One provision of the political settlement negotiated at Yalta guaranteed the return of democratic institutions to the Russian-occupied countries of Eastern Europe. Instead Joseph Stalin installed repressive regimes responsible only to his whims as undisputed dictator of the Soviet Union. After years of depredation, the unfortunate citizens of these lands now found themselves stripped of their basic freedoms and isolated from the world community. In his 1946 address at Westminster College, Missouri, Winston Churchill summed up our collective anxieties regarding this sad state of affairs with the following statement. "From Stettin in the Baltic to Trieste in the Adriatic, an **iron curtain** has descended across the continent." These two short words created such a staggering impact that, in the decades to follow, **iron curtain** became the automatic adjunct to any and all references concerning the Soviet Union and her subjugated satellite nations.

Shortly after World War II drew to a close, communism not only triumphed in China and North Korea but threatened to spread throughout most of Asia. America's foreign policy response, which was destined to achieve only limited success, became one of containment within the borders of the copycat **bamboo curtain.**

Buck
The Buck Stops Here
Passing the Buck

Whenever we ask friends for temporary loans our requests are invariably phrased in terms of a certain number of **bucks**. This short but efficient word came from gambling saloons where a token or **buck** was placed in front of the individual whose turn it was to deal next. In 1871 a United States mint began operating in Carson City, Nevada, after which **bucks** became synonymous with the silver dollars that replaced them.

Regardless of one's politics, the death of President Franklin D. Roosevelt in the spring of 1945 came as a major shock to most Americans. Because of his thirteen-year tenure, Roosevelt was the only president many citizens had ever known, making his loss seem so much more personal. Roosevelt's successor, Harry S. Truman, was neither well known nor highly regarded. Luckily the pessimists were wrong and President Truman's ability and willingness to make difficult decisions earned him a superior rating in our history books.

Since he loved poker Truman knew that a **buck** was not a dollar but an indication that someone would eventually have to deal. After a major squabble broke out among his advisors regarding a convenient depository for certain unresolved problems, President Truman abruptly ended all argument with his now famous statement that **the buck stops here**.

Throughout our daily lives we join President Truman in conceding that **the buck stops here** once we realize that certain responsibilities can no longer be avoided. Until that point in time is reached we are, however, not above indulging ourselves in the time honored practice of **passing the buck**.

Boondocks
Boot Camp
Leatherneck
Boondoggle

On May 1, 1898, Admiral Dewey sank the Spanish fleet in Manila Bay, adding the Philippine Islands to the growing American empire and setting the stage for a US military presence that was to last for almost a century. At the time, Spanish was the predominant language, although a large number of native dialects were also in general use. Our servicemen soon came into contact with one called Tagalog which, along with English, eventually became one of the country's two official languages.

The word for mountain in this native tongue was "bandok." Corrupted to **boondock** and adding an s, our soldiers and sailors began using it as a generic term for describing remote areas or terrain. **Boondocks** remained virtually unknown outside of military circles until a tragic training accident occurred in an inaccessible area of our South Carolina **leatherneck boot camp**. A major investigation followed, in the course of which **boondocks** was so prominently featured that it became a standard part of our vocabulary.

Veteran sailors used to take great pride in their ability to scrub decks in bare feet regardless of the weather. New recruits were usually less enthusiastic and tended to purchase rubber boots, earning for themselves the nickname of "rubber boot sailors." Boots and recruits became one and the same in navy lingo, a notion that eventually spread to the navy's Marine Corps division, causing their training facilities to be called **boot camps**.

For reasons lost to posterity marine dress tunics in the 1880s included a strip of leather sewn into the collar. This uncomfortable garment was soon replaced but not before bestowing upon current, as well as future generations of marines, the tough-sounding title of **leatherneck**.

Uniforms worn by the Boy Scouts once boasted an equally useless leather thong christened a **boondoggle** by scout troop leader Robert Link. The imaginative new word not only survived, but flourished for the purpose of describing and pinpointing the existence of unnecessary and expensive projects foisted on an unsuspecting public by their bureaucratic masters.

Abbreviations and Initials as Words

They creep stealthily and unnoticed into our speech patterns and, with the passage of time, are transformed into firmly entrenched words. Only a limited sampling is offered here since any comprehensive list of initials and abbreviations fitting this description would fill volumes.

A.D.	*Anno Domini*
	(Latin: in the year of our Lord)
A-OK	One step better than just okay
A.M.	*Ante meridiem*
	(Latin: before noon)
ASAP	As soon as possible
AWOL	Absent without leave
B.C.	Before Christ
BVDs	Initials of 1876 underwear manufacturers
	Bradley, Voorhies and Day
CD	Compact disk or certificate of deposit
COP	Constable on patrol
D-day	Decision day
FLAK	*Flieger abwehr kanone*
	(German: anti-aircraft defense gun)
Gestapo	*Geheime Staats Polizei*
	(German: secret state police)
GOP	Grand Old Party
	(1887 nickname for the Republican Party)
IOU	I owe you
IRS	Internal Revenue Service
KP	Kitchen clean up or "police"
K-ration	Named after Ancel Keys, K-ration inventor
Mayday	*M'aidez*
	(French: help me)
MIG	All Russian fighter aircraft honor designers,
	Mikoyan and Gurevitch
Nazi	*National Sozialist*
	(German: National Socialist Party)
PC	Personal computer

PDQ	Pretty darn quick. Attributed to comedian Daniel Maguinnis
P.M.	*Post meridium* (Latin: after noon)
PS	*Post scriptum* (Latin: afterthought)
QED	*Quod erat demonstrandum* (Latin: that which was to be demonstrated)
QT(on the)	In confidence or quietly
R & R	Rest and recreation (Dates from the Korean War)
RSVP	*Respondez, s'ill vous plait* (French: please reply)
SNAFU	Situation normal, all fouled up (from WW II)
SOS	Does not mean "save our souls" but is easily transmitted. Internationally adopted in 1908
SS	*Schutzstaffel* (German: Elite guard of Nazi police outfitted with "black-shirt" uniforms).
Stalag	*Stammlager* (German: prison camp)
Tip	To insure promptness
U-boat	*Unterseeboot* (German: undersea boat)
UFO	Unidentified flying object
VIP	Very important person

Here's Mud in Your Eye
Winning Hands Down
Also Ran
Under the Wire
On the Nose
Hold Your Horses
Come a Cropper

Offering a toast of "**here's mud in your eye**" is actually a very egotistical exercise. The expression comes from the horse racing world where front runners often kick mud in the eyes of horses following closely behind. Your overture is thus most inconsiderate, implying that you see yourself as top dog with everyone else assuming a secondary position.

Not infrequently jockeys find themselves so far out front that a reduction of pace makes sense for animal and rider alike. This is accomplished by simply lowering one's hands and loosening the reins, the inevitable outcome of which is **winning hands down**.

Newspapers used to publish entries finishing out of the money as **also ran**. It seems that all of us have acquaintances who, because of bad luck, lack of talent, or just plain laziness, spend their entire existence in the category of an **also ran**.

Races are monitored by electronic beams resembling wires when viewed on photographs and often depict two or more horses straining to place their noses **under the wire**. When deadlines loom and important projects are completed just **under the wire**, we sometimes end up bearing a close resemblance to our exhausted equine friends. Since photo-finishes are commonplace, one can also readily understand why bets are placed **on the nose** as opposed to the whole animal.

At one time harness racing constituted a major form of entertainment at country fairs, even though the local nature of these events precluded the presence of experienced riders. Novices failing to keep their mounts under control precipitated numerous false starts, causing frustrated spectators to shout "**hold your horses**." Racing event competence has certainly improved over the years, but we still beseech individuals displaying impetuous or impatient natures to **hold your horses**.

Come a cropper describes the fate of jockeys parting company from their mounts during steeplechase jumps. While this usage is more popular in England than the United States, racing fans on both sides of the pond agree that when everything goes wrong at the same time, those at the receiving end have **come a cropper**.

Keep Your Powder Dry
Keep Your Cool
Lock, Stock, and Barrel
Shot His Wad
Going Off Half Cocked
A Flash in the Pan
Biting the Bullet

America's love affair with the gun is undoubtedly related to our instinctive yearning for the frontier days, when survival often depended on proficiency in the use of firearms. Consequently, it should come as no great surprise that our language became saturated with terminology derived from weapons and their components.

The first reported public exhortation to **keep your powder dry** was probably made by Oliver Cromwell at the onset of England's 1642 civil war. Cromwell's appeal transcended the obvious fact that muskets would be rendered useless if gunpowder was improperly protected from the elements. His real intent was to steady unseasoned troops by urging them not to panic, and thus unwittingly presented us with the modern version of **keep your powder dry** i.e., "**keep your cool**."

The components of most firearms may be broken down into three categories: firing mechanisms or locks, wooden stocks, and barrels. Owning something **lock, stock, and barrel** has therefore come to indicate that one's possession of an enterprise or a physical object is complete in all respects.

Preparing primitive weapons for use required insertion of powder, followed by a wad and a lead ball. Finally, a ramrod tamped the entire arrangement securely into place, after which the hammer was pulled backwards to its furthest extension. Upon discharge the wad, having served its purpose of securing powder and shot, was ejected a short distance from the muzzle while the ball theoretically found its target. Although we must stretch our imagination somewhat to envision the parallel, individuals who have exhausted their resources or opportunities are likewise considered to have **shot their wad**. Since the external hammers of these muzzle loading rifles were not ready for discharge in a half cocked position, it also seems fitting that we accuse those displaying a propensity for acting prematurely of **going off half cocked**.

Improper attention to the loading sequence usually resulted in nothing more than a flare up in a small indentation or "pan" attached to the barrel's side. Because misfires occurred quite regularly, we are therefore quick to judge that it was just **a flash in the pan** whenever anyone's performance fades after a strong start.

Prior to the twentieth century, medical help on battlefields was almost non-existent. Amputations for controlling the spread of gangrene were commonplace, and even then more soldiers died from infections than wounds. Usually only partially effective whisky or rum was available as an anesthetic, requiring the placement of a lead bullet between soldiers' teeth to keep tongues from being bitten off during operations. Their ordeals were so excruciating that subsequent generations appropriated **biting the bullet** as a figure of speech for acknowledging that an agonizing decision can no longer be avoided or postponed.

Between the Devil and the Deep Blue Sea
Come Hell or High Water
Between a Rock and a Hard Place
On the Horns of a Dilemma

Sailing ships have always had unusual names for their many components, and the designation of "devil" for the first plank above the water line was no exception. Since hot tar and cold sea water were incompatible, ships had to be canted far over to one side before repairs to this crucial area could proceed. If port facilities were unavailable, the job had to be done while underway, requiring the power of a strong, steady wind.

Seamen chosen for this dangerous work found themselves in a most precarious position. Working in close proximity to the ship's bottom, they found themselves stationed **between the devil and the deep blue sea**. Quick repair jobs minimized the danger but also placed them **on the horns of a dilemma** in that dissatisfied captains were not above demanding repeat performances. Generally speaking, fear of subsequent trips to a region categorized as hell on earth motivated sailors to discharge this duty properly **come hell or high water**. The hell was self evident while any loss of wind provided the high water. Not to be outdone, landlubbers coined the companion phrase **between a rock and a hard place** for describing embarrassment suffered by those ensnared by compromising circumstances.

Dilemma comes from a combination of two Greek words; "*di*" meaning two and "*lemma*" indicating something taken for granted. The word *dilemma* therefore describes situations requiring a choice between two different but equally logical sets of options. A strong likelihood exists of getting stuck no matter what decision one makes, which is why we associate dilemmas with the image of two sharp horns.

Combining the various segments of this intellectual linguistic exercise provides us with **on the horns of a dilemma**. One should note that **on the horns of a dilemma, between the devil and the deep blue sea**, and **between a rock and a hard place** are all used to describe identical circumstances, despite the varied backgrounds of their origins.

Pommies
Kangaroo Court
Shanghaied
Turning the Tables

Oriental explorers may have discovered the Australian Continent in the thirteenth century, but the first colonists arrived only after Captain James Cook planted his Union Jack near Botany Bay in 1770. Shortly thereafter Great Britain selected this remote territory as a suitable dumping ground for convicts. The original settlers were therefore required to accept "Prisoners of Mother England," (POMEs), or **Pommies** in today's vernacular, and Port Jackson became a penal colony, whose inhabitants became proficient in the twin arts of self-government and the dispensation of frontier justice.

Apprehended suspects faced hastily convened courts which frequently leaped to rapid conclusions regarding innocence or guilt. Taking a cue from the appealing and fast moving marsupials of the region, the rest of the world soon decided that all examples of instant justice emanated from **kangaroo courts.**

One famous instance of **kangaroo court** mania occurred during the Korean War. Some one hundred thousand Chinese and North Korean soldiers, along with numerous civilians who had been **shanghaied** into military service, were interned in UN prison camps. Many of these captives resisted China's demand of forced repatriation to their respective homelands. Others, who remained fanatically dedicated to the communist cause, seized the internment camps on Kojedo Island and organized **kangaroo courts** in order to determine their fellow inmates' loyalties. Those unfortunate enough to be accused of improper thinking faced the prospect of assembly line conviction and execution. UN units eventually regained control through the use of armed force but not before numerous death penalties had been imposed and carried out.

Several centuries before these events took place, Britain's Royal Navy used press gangs to raid communities for young men. Unlucky volunteers were read the articles of war and told that any lack of cooperation meant banishment to Shanghai, a place so distant as to preclude the possibility of ever seeing home again. In spite of this threat, life in Shanghai was exciting, and departing vessels often found themselves so short handed that unwary sailors were routinely drugged and **shanghaied** to serve yet another set of masters.

There were undoubtedly many recorded instances whereby **shanghaied** individuals **turned the tables** on their oppressors by escaping and rejoining family and friends. Throughout history, wealthy men have criticized their wives' spending habits while engaged in their own passion for collecting expensive antique tables. Speculation exists that in self defense the fairer sex must have, at some point in time, **turned the tables** on their husbands by making them turn around and face their own extravagant purchases.

Biblical Colloquialisms

The Bible offers a vast array of material which is so commonly used and universally understood that additional comments would be superfluous. Readers seeking further enlightenment have at their disposal the most illuminating reference source of all time: the Bible itself.

A little bird told me	Ecclesiastics 10:20
A millstone around one's neck	Matthew 18:6
Apple of one's eye	Deuteronomy. 32:10
As one man	Judges 10:8
At sixes and sevens	Job 5:19
Beating swords into plowshares	Isaiah 2:4
Be of good cheer	Matthew 14:27
Blind leading the blind	Matthew 15:14
By the skin of my teeth	Job 19:20
Casting pearls before swine	Matthew 7:6
Climb (ing) the wall	Joel 2:7
Crying in the wilderness (a voice)	Isaiah 40:3
Dead letter	Corinthians 3:6
Divide and conquer	Matthew 12:25
Divide the spoils	Isaiah 9:3
Doubting Thomas	John 20:24-29
Drop in the bucket	Isaiah 40:12
Eleventh hour	Matthew 20:1-16
Evil eye	Matthew 20:15
Eye for an eye	Exodus 23:25
Fall by the wayside	Matthew 13:1
Fall from grace	Galatians 5:4
Far be it from me	Job 34:10
Feet of clay	Daniel 2:31-32
Filthy lucre	Timothy 3:5
Flesh and blood	Matthew 16:17
Fly in the ointment	Ecclesiastics 10:1
Forbidden fruit	Genesis 8:9
Four corners of the earth	Revelation 7:1
Gather ye rosebuds while ye may	Solomon 2:8

Girding one's loins	Proverbs 31:17
Giving up the ghost	Job 14:10
Good Samaritan	Luke 30:30-37
Handwriting on the wall	Daniel 5:5
Hiding one's light under a bushel	Matthew 5:14-15
His days are numbered	Daniel 5:26
Hope against hope	Romans 4:18
I am not my brother's keeper	Genesis 8:9
In his cups	Esdras 3:22
In the twinkling of an eye	Corinth. 15:51
Kill the fatted calf	Luke 15:23-24
Labor of love	Thessalonians. 2:3
Land of milk and honey	Exodus 3:8
Last gasp	Maccabees 7:9
Left hand doesn't know what the right hand is doing	Matthew 6:3
Love of money is the root of all evil	Timothy 6:10
Making one's hair stand on end	Job 4:13-14
Man after my own heart	Samuel 13:13-14
Man of few words	Ecclesiastics 5:2
Many are called but few are chosen	Matthew 22:1-14
Mark my words	Isaiah 28:23
No rest for the wicked (weary)	Isaiah 48:22
Nothing new under the sun	Ecclesiastics 1:9
Patience of Job	Job 16:2
Prophet without honor	Matthew 13:57
Salt of the earth	Matthew 5:13
Separate the wheat from the chaff	Matthew 3:12
Sick as a dog	Proverbs 26:11
Sign of the times	Matthew 3:16
Slow to anger	James 1:19-20
Speak for yourself	Acts 26:1
The race is not to the swift	Ecclesiastics 9:11
The spirit is willing but the flesh is weak	Matthew 26:41
The staff of life	Isaiah 3:1
Thorn in one's side	Corinth. 12:7
Turning the other cheek	Matthew 5:39
Wages of sin	Romans 6:23

Washing one's hands of the matter	Matthew 27:24
Way of all flesh	Kings 2:2
Wheels within wheels	Ezekiell 16
Wolf in sheep's clothing	Matthew 7:15

Posh
Putting on the Dog
Dressed to the Nines
Gilding the Lily

Evidence suggests that in 1380 B.C. an Egyptian pharaoh named Seti the 1st connected the Mediterranean and Red Seas with a canal branching off from the Nile River. Soon thereafter his project fell into disrepair and was abandoned. Successive rulers periodically attempted to replicate Seti's feat and, although some measure of success was achieved, no permanent water route was established until the 1860s when the necessary combination of technical ability and a favorable political climate finally arrived. A modern waterway was begun, and by 1869 Ferdinand deLesseps, a French engineer destined to suffer failure in Panama, completed his 100 - mile-long Suez Canal.

Officers and other ranks of the British army could now be shipped to India and back at a greatly reduced cost. Depending on which leg of the journey was involved, frequent travelers alleviated their boredom with discussions as to which side of the ship offered the greatest refuge from the extreme heat. A consensus eventually developed that one's cabin should be on the port side going out and the starboard side returning home so as to take advantage of the prevailing, cooling winds. "Port out, starboard home" became the byword, and **posh**, the abbreviated form of this requirement, entered our vocabulary as the ultimate superior accommodation.

America's post-Civil War industrialization created wealth on a scale that has seldom been equaled. Our newly emerging upper crust passed the time by popularizing new words such as **posh** and competing with one another in the creation of new fashions. These efforts allowed ladies to sally forth outfitted up to their eyes with the latest styles. Years ago the plural of eye was first eyne and then nine, a linguistic evolution permitting us to **dress to the nines**. Well-appointed socialites were often accompanied by small lap dogs. These nasty, pampered beasts resembled small fur coats, attended their mistresses' various functions, and left the impression that they might as well be part of one's wardrobe. Less affluent citizens watched these proceedings in silent wonder. Should they, however, attempt to emulate the antics of the rich and famous, their peers might castigate them for **putting on the dog** or **gilding the lily**.

In Shakespeare's *King John*, a second coronation takes place for the purpose of consolidating a rather weak claim to the throne. Lord Salisbury later scathingly describes this event in terms of painting or **gilding a lily**. While few of us are committed to political power struggles as a way of life, we have retained our propensity for **gilding the lily** whenever irresistible occasions present themselves.

The Cut of His Jib
Armed to the Teeth
On the Spot

The flow of history dictates that all nations must submit to a continuous cycle of friends, enemies, alliances, and entanglements. Accordingly, military forces will surely continue performing their traditional role of enforcing national foreign policy objectives.

Conflicts have in the past, and will undoubtedly remain in the future, an inevitable by-product of this task. One prerequisite of winning battles, and ultimately wars, has always been that opposing military units be quickly and accurately identified. Throughout the centuries sailing ships were usually afforded ample time for guessing an approaching vessel's intent, although accurate identification was often problematic. Flags tended to be hidden or falsely displayed, and the captain's entire technological arsenal was limited to a telescope.

Savvy commanders were able to bolster their knowledge by studying a potential opponent's jib. British ships tended to perform well with one such sail, while Frenchmen seemed to prefer two and the Dutch usually managed without any. After carefully analyzing the rigging of a suspicious vessel, the captain might remark to his fellow officers that he didn't like **the cut of his jib**. Concerns regarding jibs are currently confined to recreational sailors, which is not to say we have given up on voicing similar opinions upon being approached by anyone giving us cause for mistrust.

Ships preparing to engage each other in combat did not necessarily belong to the navies of warring factions. Governments frequently sanctioned the use of privately owned vessels for the purpose of preying on another country's merchant fleet. Complimenting this form of official piracy was the ongoing threat posed by the real McCoy.

Buccaneers and privateers secured their spoils by coming alongside crippled victims and swinging themselves on board using ropes attached to their own rigging. Festooned with weapons, some of which were clenched in their jaws, they arrived **armed to the teeth**. This rather dramatic image survived the ages and has been transferred to our modern societies, which tend to be **armed**

to the teeth on a permanent basis.

Professional pirates took great delight in their murderous activities and also used Draconian measures for maintaining internal discipline. Death penalty decisions were announced by presenting the condemned with the ace of spades or "spot." Occasionally, unfortunate combinations of bad judgment, timing, or luck place us **on the spot** as well, although seldom with terminal results.

Rub the Wrong Way
Soothing Ruffled Feathers
Pouring Oil on Troubled Waters

At one time small armies of servants continuously polished and scrubbed the beautifully grained wooden floors so prominently featured in our stately homes. Careless application of scouring materials against, rather than with, the grain served to produce both dirty streaks and home owner's ire because the wood had been **rubbed the wrong way**.

Whenever roosters or peacocks are upset, their hackles, or neck feathers, tend to rise. Other birds express similar emotions by ruffling their feathers until the crisis passes. Despite the physical impossibilities involved, individuals who have been **rubbed the wrong way** are generally mollified only after friends **soothe their ruffled feathers** by **pouring oil on the troubled waters**.

Many centuries ago a Chinese junk transporting fish oil was caught in a violent tropical storm. Resigned to their doom, captain and crew were astonished to find themselves surrounded by calm water even though the storm continued raging about them with unabated fury. Peering over the side, they discovered that powerful waves had broken open a cargo hold and that escaping fish oil was somehow taming the nearby waves. While no one understood this phenomena, accurate observations were recorded and passed on to future generations.

Years later scientists discovered that strong winds create large waves from small ones by whipping froth off their tops, and that continuous wind action possesses the potential for creating truly gigantic monsters. Further research revealed that application of oil disrupts this chain reaction since its viscosity prevents the wind from gaining traction on the water.

Until recent times, ships routinely carried oil for dumping overboard in storm related emergencies. Environmental concerns have outlawed this practice, forcing us to confine our custom of **pouring oil on troubled waters** to the resolution of controversial situations and the arbitration of disputes.

Kilroy Was Here
Brain Trust
Head Honcho
Kamikaze
Blockbuster
Take-Home Pay
Dear John Letter
That's All She Wrote

World War II provided us with a rare example of a written, as opposed to spoken, colloquialism. American GIs advancing through Europe's ruined cities and U.S. Marines storming Pacific island beaches frequently encountered signs proclaiming that **Kilroy was here**, shattering their belief that they had been the first to transverse this dangerous terrain. Persistent Kilroy identification efforts came to naught and years passed before dogged research finally revealed Kilroy's origin. It appears that throughout the war years James Kilroy, a military equipment inspector in the Quincy, Massachusetts, naval shipyard, habitually chalked **Kilroy was here** on all items passing his scrutiny. Soldiers and equipment routinely traveled together on long, boring voyages, giving our service men ample time to discover and store away for future use the notion that **Kilroy was here**.

When President Roosevelt took stock of his military options in the fall of 1939, he discovered that even the Netherlands surpassed the United States in number of active-duty troops. This remarkable revelation galvanized Roosevelt into organizing the National Defense Advisory Commission, a seven man **brain trust** which became responsible for remedying America's military deficiencies. This popular description for any panel of experts sprung from the fertile imagination of *New York Times* reporter James Kieran, who described the collective efforts of F.D.R.'s advisors throughout his 1932 presidential campaign as a **brain trust**.

The English language's remarkable flexibility allows it to absorb a plethora of words from friend and foe alike. **Hancho** and **kamikaze**, Japanese for "squad commander" and "wind of the gods" or "divine wind," entered our lexicon during what most senior citizens refer as "the war." **Head honcho** is now interchangeable with top dog, while **kamikaze** alludes to the self-destructive nature of those associated with fanatical causes.

Towards the end of World War II Japan's position had become so precarious that she employed **kamikaze** suicide planes in a last ditch effort to stem America's advancing tide of naval power. The devastating physiological effects created by this terrifying new form of warfare were nevertheless overcome, and, unlike the year 1281 when a **kamikaze** or "wind of the gods" destroyed an invading Mongol fleet, the land of the rising sun was soon forced to surrender.

Well worn expressions such as **blockbuster**, **take-home pay**, **dear John letter**, and **that's all she wrote** also emerged from the turbulent '30s and '40s. **Blockbusters** were huge bombs weighing up to ten tons which were capable of leveling entire city blocks. The New Deal's introduction of payroll deductions for taxes and social programs slimmed down American paychecks into **take-home pay**. War-time romances were tenuous affairs at best, and after an unknown soldier named John was rejected by mail, similar epistles received by other servicemen became **dear John letters**. Sympathetic friends inquiring after additional news were often rebuffed with **that's all she wrote**, a statement of fact which quickly gained currency with cynics and habitual pessimists for use in reinforcing negative comments covering a wide array of subjects.

Frog in Your Throat

Whenever someone appears to be hoarse or is having difficulty speaking clearly, we are tempted to ask if they have a **frog in their throat**. This possibility is not really as strange as it sounds and can be traced to Elizabethan England.

We must first, however, go back to ancient times in order to truly appreciate the role our little green friends have played throughout history. In those days the application of frogs, either dead or alive, to various parts of the body was thought to constitute a sure cure for a large variety of illnesses.

As time went by, even more remarkable uses for the species Rana gained favor. Drowning a frog in oil and massaging one's body with the resulting ointment were thought to alleviate fevers. Arthritis could be conquered if one would only place live frogs on the appropriate areas. Rinsing the mouth with frog soup might eventually cure toothaches, while skin problems were treatable by breathing the ashes of cremated baby frogs.

By Shakespeare's time acting had become such an important profession that no expense was spared when performers developed sore throats. If all else failed a live frog was produced, held by one leg, and moved slowly up and down the afflicted area. The supposedly beneficial secretions emanating from the frog's skin undoubtedly tasted so terrible that many patients quickly pronounced themselves cured.

The nineteenth century ushered in a further expansion of the frog's magical power. A live specimen permanently attached to one's head was prescribed for eye infections. Intestinal ailments theoretically succumbed after ingesting frog broth, while frog meat was often recommended to counter miscellaneous afflictions.

Modern research has shown that these early attempts to use frogs for medical purposes were not totally off the mark. Several South American species are endowed with powerful poisons that may someday help in the treatment of heart disease. Frog skins also contain a whole array of previously unknown chemicals, some of which have already been tested as possible cures for our most stubborn diseases.

Unfortunately for both science and nature, frogs are extremely sensitive to environmental change. As such they are disappearing at an alarming rate, creating the distinct possibility that future generations will have to read about these wonderful creatures in books, along with the American passenger pigeon and the dodo bird.

You Can Run but You Can't Hide
Hitting Below the Belt
Straight from the Shoulder
Come up to Scratch
Throw in the Towel
Throw in the Sponge
Put up Your Dukes

During Joe Louis and Billy Conn's first boxing match in 1941, Conn stayed ahead on point count through twelve rounds and Louis barely managed a last minute knock out win. Prior to a 1946 rematch, Conn, who was not only fleet of foot but also twenty pounds lighter, boastfully pronounced he could run circles around his opponent. Joe Louis took these antics in stride, responding with **he can run but he can't hide**. Billy Conn did indeed run for seven rounds, but there really was no place to hide, and a well placed glove in round eight settled the issue once and for all. Although generic usage has replaced "he" with "you," the point remains valid: life is replete with problems from which **you can run but not hide**.

Although modern day boxing has often been criticized as a brutal, uncivilized sport, this form of entertainment used to be even less humane. Prior to the 1867 acceptance of the Marquis of Queensberry's rules, fighters used bare knuckles, rounds were unlimited in number, and hitting any part of the body was permitted. Because of the Marquis' perseverance, today's boxers use gloves, fight limited rounds, and are not allowed to hit below the belt. For obvious reasons this last change was so important that those taking cheap shots or breaking with accepted social behavior are invariably reprimanded for **hitting below the belt**.

The most powerful blow a fighter can unleash uses his body weight to enhance momentum and comes straight from his shoulder. Since most of us prefer hearing unpleasant tidings without reservations, we have learned to plead with bearers of bad news for disclosure **straight from the shoulder**.

Failure to **come up to scratch** suggests substandard performance, as was once exemplified by prize fighters conceding matches after being unable to cross lines scratched in the dirt.

Today's prizefighter managers signal surrender by throwing towels or sponges into the ring, a practice that also allows us to mentally **throw in the towel** or **throw in the sponge** whenever life's vicissitudes threaten to overwhelm us.

Physical confrontations are often preceded by challenges to **put up your dukes**. Frederick, the second son of George III and also the Duke of York, enjoyed participation in and observation of sporting events, with special emphasis on boxing. Because of Frederick's popularity, boxers referred to their fists as "dukes," and two centuries later we steadfastly **put up our dukes** whenever our honor requires defending.

Bobby
Raining Cats and Dogs
Can't Hold a Candle To
The Game is Not Worth the Candle

Those of us residing in large cities often find it fashionable to complain about taxes, crime, and our deteriorating infrastructure. In truth we should be thanking our lucky stars for the privilege of living in the twentieth century. Starting in the late 1600s, Europe's urban centers entered a period of rapid growth brought on by the emerging industrial revolution. Public services we now take for granted did not exist and most citizens endured conditions of indescribable squalor, while epidemics and fires ravaged rich and poor with equal savagery.

Just imagine the City of London functioning without an organized constabulary until 1828, when future English Prime Minister Sir Robert Peel created the London Metropolitan Police Force. Members of this establishment started out as "peelers" but later , as a take off on Sir Robert's nickname, became familiar to millions of London tourists as **bobbies**.

In the not too distant past, almost all cities lacked sewers, drainage facilities, and trash collection services. Garbage, which often included dead cats and dogs, was thrown out of windows along with other, even more unsavory wastes. Heavy rainstorms periodically swept such volumes of this disgusting mess through the streets that it appeared to have come from the heavens. In due course the establishment of proper municipal services ended this phenomena, but we have nevertheless retained our propensity for equating heavy downpours with **raining cats and dogs**.

Before the advent of gas street lighting, citizens returning home after dark required the guidance of young boys holding candles. Their profession was held in such low esteem that it became natural, upon comparing the talents of two individuals, to announce that one of them **can't hold a candle to** the other. It is noteworthy that **raining cats and dogs** and **can't hold a candle to** have remained a part of our language, even though the conditions that spawned their creation have long since disappeared.

City dwellers of those bygone days enjoyed nightly games of

chance with losers traditionally paying for the essential and not inexpensive candles. This is why disheartened souls, fed up with life's vicissitudes, occasionally venture that **the game is not worth the candle**.

Knock on Wood
Touch Wood
Scapegoat
Keep Your Fingers Crossed

Most colloquialisms can be attributed to one reasonably acceptable source. In the case of **knock on wood**, two distinct origins exists, and the reader will just have to make his or her choice.

Many ancient cultures, including those of native American Indian tribes, believed that trees were possessed by either good or evil spirits and possibly a combination of both. These widely separated societies instinctively feared Earth's foreboding, primeval forests which then blanketed major portions of our planet. Lacking communication, they nevertheless found a common solution to their inbred fears by knocking on tree trunks to both appease evil spirits and please good ones. Climatic changes and human needs eventually denuded large areas of their original growth, but **knocking on wood** survives as a precursor of good fortune.

In medieval times, vendors roamed the countryside peddling what they claimed to be portions of Jesus' true cross. Small pieces of this questionable commodity could be acquired quite cheaply, while those without means were allowed to **touch wood**, indicating their devotion to God. Even today we are not always skeptical when presented with such an opportunity, as evidenced by the substantial sum recently paid at an European auction for what was purported to be just such a holy relic. While few of us possess enough conviction, courage, and excess funds for investments of this nature, our superstitious past remains alive and well as we continue to seek out wooden objects to touch for good luck.

Early Christians living under Rome's succession of despotic emperors often became **scapegoats** for that society's many ills. Practicing their faith surreptitiously lest they receive invitations to dine with the lions, making the sign of the cross was sometimes downsized to crossing one's fingers. Christianity ultimately triumphed over its oppressors, and **keep your fingers crossed** joined **knock on wood** and **touching wood** as fortuitous gestures.

New religions invariably incorporate portions of previously established faiths in order to vanquish basic resistance to change.

For example, the idea of one God proved to be a difficult concept for some Roman converts to Christianity, a problem that was neatly solved by the invention of Saints. We should also recognize that the practice of absolving one's sins originated with Judaism, not Christianity, since Judaism called for two goats to be selected for sacrifice on the Day of Atonement. One animal was put to death while the other was allowed to escape after the high priest confessed the sins of his people in its presence. The escaped goat, or **scapegoat**, disappeared to regions unknown, taking along and dispersing everyone's collective sins to the winds. The goat definitely received a bum rap, as do individuals in our own society who become **scapegoats** for the shortcomings of others.

An Ax to Grind
Keep Your Nose to the Grindstone
Bury the Hatchet
Underdog
Top Dog
Fly off the Handle

Benjamin Franklin's remarkable abilities, as well as the happy coincidence that his life span overlapped the transition from British rule to American self government, allowed him to carve a unique niche in our country's history. Franklin's many qualities included an outstanding work ethic, leading us to credit him with inventing **an ax to grind** for describing persons exhibiting ulterior motives, and **keep your nose to the grindstone** as a painful reminder that, once started, projects should be satisfactorily concluded.

Few citizens realize that portions of our Constitution drew sustenance from covenants developed by native American Indians. While the Indian concept of **burying the hatchet** was not embodied in the Constitution, politicians are by necessity instinctively drawn to this philosophy. Hatchets, or tomahawks, not only served as weapons and implements but also constituted important symbols for all Indian tribes. Peace ceremonies were often solemnized by **burying the hatchets** belonging to warring chiefs, although a major drawback to this custom was that digging them up provided hotheads with instant declarations of war.

America's earliest pioneers utilized adzes to shape logs and boards for constructing dwellings, and examples of their impressive labors may still be viewed in some of our older homes. Some years later two man saws made their debut, permitting more efficient conversion of trees to planks. This new technology required the digging of elongated pits over which logs were placed in a lengthwise position. One workman then entered the pit while his partner straddled the operation from above. Laborers possessing marginal physical attributes invariably ended up under the log and became **underdogs**, a label since expanded to include people and teams judged to be the weakest or least favored. Since language rarely develops lopsidedly, the strongest log sawing partners invented, and now share with all achievers of important positions, the title of **top dog**.

Axes consist of long wooden handles, steel heads, and wedges used to secure the tool's business end. Combining a vigorous swing with an improperly attached wedge provides the potential for an ax's head to **fly off the handle**. Due to the dangerous aspects associated with this possibility, we have taken to portraying individuals burdened with uncontrollable tempers as prone to **fly off the handle**.

William Shakespeare's Contribution

A cat has nine lives
Good king of cats, nothing but one of your nine lives.
Romeo and Juliet: Act III Scene I

A cold heart
Cold-hearted towards me?
Anthony and Cleopatra: Act III Scene XIII

A lean and hungry look
Yond Cassius has a lean and hungry look.
Julius Caesar: Act I Scene II

A plague on both your houses
I am hurt, a plague o' both your houses, I am sped.
Romeo and Juliet: Act III Scene I

Alas poor Yorik, I knew him well
Alas poor Yorik, I knew him.
Hamlet: Act III Scene II

All that glitters is not gold
All that glistens is not gold.
Merchant of Venice: Act II Scene VII

By the book
A braggart, a rogue, a villain, that
fights by the book of arithmetic.
Romeo and Juliet: Act III Scene I

By the same token
By the same token, you are a bawd.
Troilus and Cassandra: Act I Scene II

Change of heart
Not changing heart with habit, I am
still attorneyed at your service.
Measure for Measure: Act V Scene I

Cheek by jowl
Follow nay, I'll go with thee cheek by jole.
A Midsummer-Night's Dream: Act II Scene II

Dead for a ducat, dead
How now! a rat? Dead for a ducat, dead.
Hamlet: Act III Scene I

Double double toil and trouble
Double, double toil and trouble;
fire burn and cauldron bubble.
Macbeth: Act IV Scene I

Eating one out of house and home
He has eaten me out of house and home: He has out
all my substinance into that fat belley of his.
Henry IV: Act I Scene I

Foot loose and fancy free
And the imperial votaress passed on
in maiden meditation, fancy free.
A Midsummer-Night's Dream: Act II Scene I

Gilding the lily
To gild refined gold, to paint the lily.
King John: Act IV Scene II

Give him the back of your hand
He put it by with the back of his hand.
Julius Caesar: Act I Scene II

Give short shrift to
Make a short shrift; he longs to see your head.
Richard III: Act III Scene IV

Go like the wind
About the wood go swifter than the wind.
A Midsummer-Night's Dream: Act III Scene II

Good night, sweet prince
Now cracks a noble heart, good night, sweet prince.

Hamlet: Act V Scene II

Green-eyed monster
It is the green eyed monster which doth mock.
Othello: Act III Scene III

Hair's breath escape
Of hair-breath scapes, the imminent deadly breach.
Othello: Act I Scene III

Heart of gold
The King's a bawcock and a heart of gold.
Henry V part 2: Act IV Scene I

Helter-skelter
And helter-skelter have I rode to thee.
Henry IV: Act V Scene I

Hoist with his own petard
For 'tis sport to have the engineer hoist with his own
petard and it shall go hard.
Hamlet: Act III Scene IV

In my mind's eye
A mote it is to trouble the mind's eye.
Hamlet: Act III Scene I

In one fell swoop
What, all my pretty chickens and
their dam, in one fell swoop?
Macbeth: Act IV Scene III

In the dumps
Why, how now, daughter Katherine! In your dumps?
The Taming of the Shrew: Act II Scene I

Innocent as a lamb
My lord, our kinsman Glouchester is as innocent from meaning
treason to our royal person as is the suckling lamb.
Henry VI Part 2: Act III Scene I

It beggars description
It beggar'd all description.
Anthony and Cleopatra: Act II Scene II

Itching palms
Let me tell you Casius, you yourself are much condemnd to have
an itching palm
Julius Caesar: Act 1, Scene III

It's all Greek to me
But for mine part, it was Greek to me.
Julius Caesar: Act I Scene II

It's an ill wind that blows no good
Not the ill wind which blows no man to good.
Henry IV: Act V Scene III

It's the be-all and the end-all
This blow might be the be-all and the end-all.
Macbeth: Act I Scene VII

Killed with kindness
This is a way to kill a wife with kindness.
The Taming of the Shrew: Act IV Scene I

Last gasp
Fight till the last gap: I will be your guard.
Henry VI Part 1 Act I Scene II

Lead by the nose
Will as tenderly led by the nose as asses are.
Othello: Act I Scene III

Leading one down the primrose path
Himself the primrose path of dalliance treads.
Hamlet: Act I Scene II

Lead on Macduff
Lay on Macduff, and damn'd be him that
first cries hold "enough!"
Macbeth: Act V Scene VIII

Lend an ear
Friends, Romans, countrymen lend me your ears.
Julius Caesar: Act III Scene I

Let slip the dogs of war
Cry havok and let slip the dogs of war.
Julius Caesar: Act III Scene I

Lily white
Most radiant Pyramus lily white of hue.
A Midsummer-Night's Dream: Act III Scene II

More honored in the breach than the observance
And to the manor born, it is a custom more honored in the breach than the observance.
Hamlet: Act I Scene IV

My kingdom for a horse
A horse, a horse, my kingdom for a horse.
Richard III: Act V Scene IV

Neither a borrower nor a lender be
Neither a borrower nor a lender be, for loan oft loses both itself and friend.
Hamlet: Act I Scene III

Once more into the breach
Once more into the breach, dear friends, once more.
Henry V part 2: Act III Scene 1

Out, damned spot, out
Out, damned spot, out same, I say!
Macbeth: Act V Scene I

Post haste
Write from us to him: post-post haste.
Othello: Act I Scene III

Pound of flesh
A pound of a man's flesh taken from a man.
Merchant of Venice: Act I Scene III

Salad days
My salad days when I was green in judgment.
Anthony and Cleopatra: Act I Scene V

Screw up your courage
But screw your courage to the sticking place.
Macbeth: Act I Scene VII

Set one's teeth on edge
And that would set my teeth nothing on edge.
Henry IV: Act III Scene 1

Sharper than a serpent's tooth
How sharper than a serpent's tooth it is.
King Lear: Act I Scene IV

Shuffle off this mortal coil
When we have shuffled off this mortal coil.
Hamlet: Act III Scene I

Something is rotten in the State of Denmark
Something is rotten in the State of Denmark.
Hamlet: Act I Scene IV

Standing on ceremony
Caesar, I never stood on ceremony.
Julius Caesar: Act II Scene II

Still waters run deep
Smooth runs the water where the brook is deep.
Henry VI Part 2: Act III Scene I

Suffer the slings and arrows of outrageous fortune
Whether 'tis nobler in the mind to suffer
the slings and arrows of outrageous fortune.
Hamlet: Act III Scene I

The evil that men do
The evil that men do lives after them.
Julius Caesar: Act III Scene II

The milk of human kindness
It is too full o' the milk of human kindness.
Macbeth: Act I Scene V

The time is ripe
When time is ripe, which will be suddenly.
Henry IV: Act I Scene II

The unkindest cut of all
This was the most unkindest cut of all.
Julius Caesar: Act III Scene II

The world is my oyster
Why then, the world's mine oyster.
The Merry Wives of Windsor: Act II Scene I

The worm has turned
The smallest worm will turn being trodden on.
Henry VI Part 3: Act II Scene II

To be or not to be
To be or not to be; that is the question.
Hamlet: Act III Scene I

To one's heart content
Such is the fullness of my heart's content.
Henry VI part 2: Act I Scene I

To the manner born
And to the manner born, it is a custom.
Hamlet: Act I Scene IV

Up in arms
As hating thee, are rising up in arms.
Henry IV part 2: Act IV Scene I

Wearing your heart on your sleeve
But I will wear my heart upon my sleeve.
Othello: Act I Scene III

What fools these mortals be
Lord, what fools these mortals be.
A Midsummer-Night's Dream: Act III Scene II

What the dickens
I cannot tell what the dickens his name is
my husband had of him.
Merry Wives of Windsor: Act III Scene II

What's new on the rialto
Now, what news on the Rialto.
Merchant of Venice: Act I Scene I

Wild goose chase
Nay, if thy wits run the wild goose chase.
Romeo and Juliet: Act III Scene IV

Yeoman service
It did yeoman's service.
Hamlet: Act I Scene II

It is truly remarkable that so many currently used colloqui-alisms originated with Shakespeare's literary genius. Examples such as **Screw up your courage**, **It's all Greek to me** and **Eating one out of house and home**, sound more like twentieth century inventions than products from a time when North America was still an empty, unexplored wilderness.

Uncle Sam
GI
America's Cup
John Bull

Signs posted on the outskirts of Troy, New York, proclaim that city to be the home of **Uncle Sam**. Throughout our 1812 War with Great Britain, one Samuel Wilson, whose uncle owned a meat packing plant in Troy, made his living inspecting beef purchased by the United States government for distribution to our northern forces.

At the time British and American ships were engaged in sporadic combat on Lake Champlain, a large body of water located some 100 miles to the north. Boxes of beef sent to sustain this operation were stamped with the initials "US," which quite obviously stood for "United States." Because Wilson's approval of each beef shipment was required and his first name began with an S, his peers jokingly dubbed him **Uncle Sam**.

Somehow Sam Wilson's nickname spread beyond Troy's environs, and our servicemen began designating **Uncle Sam** as the originator of all sustenance provided by their government. Around 1830 the illusion was completed by an unknown artist who created the caricature of Uncle Sam as we know him today. Sometime thereafter **GI** or "government issue" came into common use, a label that by World War II encompassed both men and supplies.

In 1870 our yacht *America* managed to win, despite shenanigans involving rule changes in midstream, a long-established sailing race heretofore dominated by Great Britain. Not only did *America* return home with a coveted trophy, but future U.S. entries extended their winning streak to the point where the event's title became **America's Cup**. Great Britain did not accept her loss of prestige graciously, and Harpers magazine capitalized on England's discomfort by depicting a smiling **Uncle Sam** mocking a scowling **John Bull**, his portly, ruddy-faced British counterpart. The incident itself was soon forgotten but not before indelibly affixing the image of **Uncle Sam**, complete with striped trousers, beard, and top hat, in the minds of the American public.

Sometime during the seventeenth century, envious Europeans endowed Britain's citizens with the mantle of *les rosbifs*, French for "beef eaters." The wealth created by England's expanding empire had provided her population the luxury of conspicuous beef consumption, while continental Europe remained mired in a dependence on swine products. Beef thus became equated with strength, cows and bulls were held in high esteem, and **John Bull** came to represent the predominant symbol of Great Britain's world power status.

Queer as a Three-Dollar Bill
Wildcatter
Derrick
Barnburner

The first United States coins were minted in 1793, but our government waited until the 1860s before creating a national paper currency. Prior to that time local banks capable of obtaining state charters were allowed to print and distribute their own money, a system that worked remarkably well due to the self-sufficient nature of most communities.

Capital for banking ventures was not necessarily raised locally, and investor protection laws required banks to publish permanent addresses for inspection purposes. Sometimes dishonest promoters acquired charters for non-existent banks, whose registered addresses turned out to be in the boondocks. Stockholders unable to locate their investments might ask the locals for directions only to be told, "oh, that's out where the wildcats live."

After the Civil War ended, our government made overtures to replace some fourteen thousand different types of bank notes issued by these institutions with its own paper money. Many citizens resisted the concept of a national currency, preferring their local monetary systems over Washington's promises. Eventually a compromise was forged whereby the new "greenbacks" were imprinted with local bank names in order to retain a sense of continuity. The new system eliminated three-dollar bills, paving the way for anything out of the ordinary or "queer" to become **queer as a three-dollar bill**.

By the turn of the century oil exploration replaced the formation of banks as the country's prime speculative activity. Unaccountably, the image of bank stockholders scouring wildcat country for their investments remained solidly entrenched in people's minds, which is why oil prospectors probing the wilderness became **wildcatters**.

Before the advent of portable drilling rigs, **wildcat** wells used wooden **derricks** from which drilling equipment was suspended. If operations panned out, these tall, majestic symbols of the oil industry were left in place, to be used for subsequent well maintenance and repairs. Godfrey Derrick, London's public hangman in the early 1600s, presided over thousands of executions during his career. Because Derrick displayed such an unusual talent for improving the efficiency of his various hanging devices, today's hoisting and lifting machines continue their functional roles as **derricks**.

In the 1850s a band of violent anti-slave activists created a new political party, calling themselves **Barnburners**. Practicing what their name implied, citizens who embraced different philosophies often found themselves minus a barn or two. Subsequent events made this group of fanatics obsolete, and their name was soon forgotten. In subsequent years **wildcatters** resurrected the **barnburner** label, first for characterizing burning or out-of-control wells and later for highlighting important hydrocarbon discoveries. Current usage has been expanded once again, allowing **barnburner** to encompass any number of significant events.

Tank
Shrapnel
Molotov Cocktail

In 1915 Winston Churchill resigned his position as First Lord of the Admiralty because of his role in the disastrous Gallipoli campaign. Wishing to remain active, this future English prime minister readily accepted command of an infantry battalion in France, where he astutely observed that Hiram Maxim's new machine guns were dramatically altering the rules of infantry warfare.

Upon returning to England, Churchill proposed the development of an armored vehicle for the purpose of providing a shield against Maxim's devastating invention. Basic requirements were the ability to traverse rough terrain, blast gaps in the enemy lines, and provide protection for both crew and following infantry. Churchill's concept was approved, and the British government, wishing to preserve secrecy, made arrangements for the machine's various components to be manufactured in widely separated locations. Workers' curiosity relating to the project was contained with the ruse that they were constructing an advanced type of water collecting **tank**.

The new weapon's contribution towards ending World War I was debatable, but its introduction unquestionably altered the conduct and tactics of all future conflicts. The arbitrary designation of **tank** was never challenged, adding yet another word to our military vocabulary.

Despite Churchill's contribution to the war effort, his name, unlike that of Henry Shrapnel and Vyacheslav Molotov, never became associated with any kind of weapon. In the early 1800s Shrapnel invented a shell which exploded while in flight, spewing a deadly hail of lead balls into enemy lines. The machine gun's unsurpassed killing power rendered Shrapnel's invention obsolete, but his name retains a military association because we always refer to fragments from exploding shells and hand grenades as **shrapnel**.

During the 1940 Finno-Soviet war, the Finns discovered that bottles of gasoline capped with burning wicks produced spectacular results when thrown at tanks. Finland blamed its current conflict on Soviet foreign minister Molotov because he had politically diffused the possibility of German intervention. In retaliation Finnish troops dubbed their home made gasoline bombs **Molotov cocktails**, which in due time became the generic name for all unsophisticated but reliable incendiary devices.

Cash on the Barrelhead
On the Cuff
Getting Down to Brass Tacks
Breaking the Ice
Hitting the Nail on the Head
Talking Turkey

While the younger generation undoubtedly enjoys today's cavernous shopping malls, old-timers must surely mourn the demise of the general store, which once offered services going far beyond anything we envision today. In addition to a wide selection of merchandise, these establishments provided space for formal meetings, social gatherings, postal services, and places by the stove for senior citizens to while away the hours.

Staples such as crackers and flour were sold directly from their shipping barrels, while unopened or turned over empty barrels served as counters and seats. Retail credit did not exist, and all purchases required payment of **cash on the barrelhead**. Concurrently, bars were ahead of their time as bartenders often recorded regular customers' unpaid consumption on their starched cuffs, a form of bookkeeping that lets us order wide varieties of goods and services **on the cuff**.

Newcomers claiming seats near the general store's pot bellied wood stove could start conversations, i.e. **break the ice**, by **getting down to brass tacks**, **hitting the nail on the head**, or by just plain **talking turkey**.

Yard goods constituted a major portion of our early retail trade, and brass tacks hammered into long boards at predetermined intervals served as quick and easily read measuring devices. This simple invention neatly circumvented the necessity of making involved calculations, and lets us admonish individuals assuming ponderous postures to stop beating about the bush and **get down to brass tacks**.

Direct, practical approaches to any subject are likened to **hitting the nail on the head**. Anyone interested in carpentry can attest to the direct, pleasant, and satisfying sound produced by solid contact between hammer and nail.

Talking turkey, an additional synonym for no-frills

conversation, is traceable to a sort of colonial Aesop's Fable, in which an Indian and a white hunter are divvying up the day's haul of crows and turkeys. When the latter repeatedly took a turkey for himself after handing the Indian a crow, the Indian reportedly **hit the nail on the head** by muttering, "you **talk turkey**, I get crow."

Cold Enough to Freeze the Balls off a Brass Monkey
Hotter Than Dutch Love

Please don't be offended should someone mention that the winter of 1994 was **cold enough to freeze the balls off a brass monkey**, as the origin of this expression is really quite harmless.

Whenever warring navies approached each other, cannon balls had to be accessible despite the vexing problems these round objects created. Salvation appeared in the form of iron trays or "monkeys," whose round indentations were spaced at exact intervals and secured the balls, enabling gunners to keep adequate supplies of ammunition on hand. For ceremonial purposes, the rather unattractive iron monkeys were replaced with ones made of brass, on which tall pyramids of iron balls were erected. No one anticipated the unequal contraction rates for iron and brass which, when combined with extremely cold weather, pushed the balls off the tray and caused comments to the effect that it was **cold enough to freeze the balls off a brass monkey**.

Understandably this expression is not often used in polite society since relatively few people are aware of its innocuous origin. Less critical circles, enjoying the graphic impression conveyed, tend to exercise no such restraint.

The opposite end of the temperature spectrum has given us **hotter than Dutch love** for describing unseasonably warm weather. Dutch colonists not only founded New Amsterdam in the early 1620s but also created additional settlements as far north as present-day Albany. During this period of expansion, they came face to face with the unique problem of having too much land and not enough settlers. Parents of young couples anticipating marriage thus realized that an inability to procreate would doom their union to economic failure. To circumvent this possibility, pre-marital cohabitation was strongly encouraged, and parental blessings were often granted only after pregnancies had been established.

No social stigma was attached to this arrangement, with the birth of children shortly after marriage being considered quite normal. We must also assume that an unusual amount of passion was released during these trial periods, resulting in the birth of both babies and the phrase **hotter than Dutch love**.

Cold Shoulder
Eating Humble Pie
The Upper Crust
Hoity Toity
Hoi Polloi

The institution of knighthood came into being because most medieval communities could not afford standing armies. Instead, young men of good character and noble birth were rewarded with knighthood after successfully completing martial arts training. Not unlike our present day ROTC programs, the newly anointed were then expected to both organize and lead in the future defense of their lord's domains.

Knights traditionally roamed the countryside with full expectations of securing first rate meals and comfortable shelter at every stopping place. Ordinary travelers also received sustenance, although their lower social standing relegated them to the stables and left over **cold shoulder** of mutton. Today's **cold shoulders** are no longer indicative of inferior status. Instead, we dispense them physically by turning away from or ignoring those who have incurred our displeasure.

Should **cold shoulder** be in short supply, weary supplicants might be forced to settle for venison entrails or "umble." In order to make this fare even remotely palatable, umble was baked into pies, allowing for the evolution of **humble pie** as a play on words. Because this concoction was so nauseous, we now confess to **eating humble pie** only after our most embarrassing judgmental errors have been disclosed to the world at large.

Knights, nobles, and even monarchs rarely hesitated in partaking of whatever hospitality was available. Protocol required that hosts show proper allegiance by serving important guests with the end or **upper crust** from each loaf of bread. Even thought the existence of this custom has faded from our collective memory, our social leaders somehow continue to exude an **upper crust** aura.

Throughout past centuries the French **upper crust** luxuriated in their castles and looked down on the **hoi polloi**, i.e. peasants, from a "haut toit" or high roof. The Anglicized version of haut toit became **hoity toity**, and since **hoity toity** and **hoi polloi** sound alike they are often erroneously interchanged. **Hoi polloi** comes from a Greek word for "many" or "masses," so that its meaning is diametrically opposed to the snobbish sounding **hoity toity**.

Boycott
Dun
Bum Rap
Draconian Measures
Bum
Bum's Rush
Bum Steer
Bummer
Your Name is Mudd

Captain Charles Boycott retired from military service in 1880 to manage property located in Ireland but owned by English landlords. Around the same time leaders of an Irish organization called the National Land League were agitating for land reform with major emphasis on ending English absentee ownership. Coincidentally, Boycott was establishing a reputation for relentless enforcement of contracts between tenant farmers and landlords in that very same category.

This unfortunate combination of circumstances started a revolution of sorts. Boycott's life was threatened, his property was destroyed, and his employees were intimidated into leaving their jobs. Townspeople refused to sell Boycott provisions and wouldn't even deliver his mail. Stories of rent strikes and violence attracted media attention, and Boycott's name became linked with the concept of using ostracization as a weapon to redress grievances. The English language gained a new word as we now **boycott** individuals, organizations, or even entire nations should they engage in activities construed to be detrimental to society's interests.

Captain Boycott had company regarding the negative preservation of his name. Joe Dun, a London bailiff from the time of Henry VIII, was so adept at extracting money from his charges that his name became associated with the art of making people pay up. At one time or another most of us have **dunned** others for unpaid loans or been **dunned** due to oversights on our part.

While Boycott and Dun probably deserved their unfavorable publicity, an Athenian legislator named Draco was less fortunate. In 621 B.C. Draco codified all of Athens's unwritten but excessively severe laws. Although Draco did not promulgate these harsh laws, history gave him a **bum rap** because **Draconian measures** have become synonymous with legal tyranny.

The word **bum** was first applied to soldiers forced to live off the land during our Civil War. Since then **bum** has expanded in scope to include, among other things, vagabonds and rear ends. **Bum's rush** describes physical expulsion involving the grasping of one's pants seat and propulsion into the street. A **bum rap** is underworld slang for a false charge, and **bum steer** indicates bad advice, while just plain **bummer** means either bad luck or unfortunate circumstances.

Your name is Mudd: i.e., you are bad and everyone is out to get you, exemplifies the unfair treatment sometimes meted out by societies caught up in bursts of irrational hysteria. In 1865 Dr. Samuel Mudd set the broken leg of a stranger subsequently identified as John Wilkes Booth. Even though not a shred of evidence linked him to the conspiracy, Dr. Mudd was sentenced to life imprisonment in the Dry Tortugas as an accomplice in the assassination of President Lincoln. His heroic services during a yellow fever epidemic earned Dr. Mudd a pardon, but another hundred years were destined to pass before his name was finally cleared by a conviction reversal signed by President Jimmy Carter.

Bought the Farm
I'm a Gone Goose
Knocked into a Cocked Hat
SNAFU

In 1994 our Republic passed its two hundred and eighteenth birthday. Even though this brief time span equals only three lifetimes, the United States has managed to embroil itself in wars with England, Mexico, Spain, Germany, Italy, Japan, China, North Korea, North Vietnam, and Iraq. Most tragic of all was our own Civil War, the memory of which haunts us even today.

Manpower requirements for our various conflicts have traditionally been satisfied by both conscription and the use of volunteers. Whenever draftees were pressed into service, many of them expressed strong desires to be almost anywhere else and longingly talked about buying a farm on which to retire from the world at large. Inevitably, some of these unhappy souls were destined to be killed in action. Subsequent reflections by comrades on each tragic loss often ended with comments that the deceased had **bought the farm**, meaning he was finally at peace. We continue to use this expression, as well as the alternative version of "he's bought it," whenever physical tragedy strikes home.

War, in spite of its accompanying tragedy and horror, does sometimes produce brief, humorous moments. One such occasion arose during our Revolutionary War after an American soldier disguised himself in coon skins and climbed a tree in order to spy on British troop dispositions. An enemy soldier spotted and raised his musket to shoot what he surmised to be the world's largest coon. The American, believing his ruse had been discovered, shouted "don't shoot, **I'm a gone coon** and will surrender." The Britisher, terrified by this large talking animal, reportedly threw down his weapon and fled for his life. Both sides thought this was so funny that the **gone coon** was quickly repatriated in a prisoner exchange without the English raising the potentially serious charge of espionage. **Gone coon** soon faded from use because it was not euphemistic enough but re-emerged in subsequent years in a more viable form as **gone goose**.

The **gone coon** episode highlighted the fact that America's first war was not always conducted on a highly professional level.

British leadership often tended towards crucial errors that were later redeemed by local militia led by popularly elected but inexperienced officers. During World War II **SNAFU** (situation normal, all fouled up) came into use, which was the equivalent of the colonial **knocked into a cocked hat**. The latter referred to the three-cornered headgear worn by our farmers turned soldier, whose leadership qualities and knowledge of military tactics often left much to be desired.

Colloquial Numbers

The magical properties of numbers are not confined to mathematics, and hopefully this offering will heighten the reader's awareness of their impact on our language.

FIRST RATE: British warships were once rated on a scale from one to six, with **first rate** reserved for vessels sporting the most decks and cannon. We now turn up our noses at anything regarded as third rate or even second rate, despite the fact that ships fitting these lower categories once constituted formidable adversaries as well.

SECOND STRING: Because symphonic orchestras' first violinists traditionally assume intermediary roles between orchestra and conductor, the importance of the second violinist or **second string** tends to be obscured. This unfair circumstance has been translated to the sports world in that the least recognized, albeit necessary, players often spend disproportionate amounts of time on the sidelines as the **second string**.

THIRD DEGREE: Freemasonry members aspiring to achieve their organization's **third degree** of Master Mason must undergo exhaustive proficiency testing. Police departments have been known to apply similar physiological pressures and even physical abuse to suspects with prior records, a practice that engenders fear of subjugation to the **third degree**.

FOUR F: Throughout World War II our Selective Service organization designated many draftees and volunteers as physically, morally, physiologically, or generally unsuitable for military service. These fortunate or unfortunate individuals, depending on their point of view, were classified as **4-F** (failure to qualify for at least one of four reasons). The **4-F** concept survived the war, becoming an onerous and judgmental label applicable to individuals lacking in physical attributes.

FIFTH WHEEL: Carriages from our pre-automotive era came equipped with extra wheels attached to their front axles. These appurtenances provided support during sharp turns but otherwise never touched the ground, providing casual observers with an impression of total uselessness. Even though relatively few people remember those bygone days, we nevertheless categorize superfluous people or physical objects as **fifth wheels**.

SIXTH SENSE: Most of us are endowed with the five senses of smell, touch, hearing, sight, and taste. A small percentage of the human race is additionally blessed, or perhaps cursed, with an indefinable ability to perceive the future, a phenomena we refer to as a **sixth sense**.

SEVENTH HEAVEN: Despite the difficult relationship between Jews and Arabs, their faiths share certain common beliefs. One such binding thread concerns the ecstatic state of mind referred to as **seventh heaven**. Islam recognizes graduated layers of heaven, and those fortunate enough to reach the final, exalted **seventh heaven** are rewarded with lives of unparalleled joy, along with opportunities to sing Allah's praises. The tenets of Judaism also reflect upon a **seventh heaven** as a region boasting spectacular light which is presided over by Abraham. Although Christian teachings espouse one heaven for all, Christ's followers occasionally join Arabs and Jews in their own version of **seventh heaven**.

BEHIND THE EIGHT BALL: Behind the eight ball originates from the game of pool and is reserved for those finding themselves in untenable positions. Rules covering variations such as "stripes & solids" and "Kelly pool" provide for loss of game or penalty points for premature sinking or interaction with the eight ball. Strategy therefore dictates that on certain occasions shots should be attempted whose sole purpose to place one's opponent **behind the eight ball**.

ON CLOUD NINE: In seventh heaven and **on cloud nine** convey identical emotions except that the latter is devoid of religious overtones. Credit for the popularization of **on cloud nine** accrues to Fibber McGee's pre-television radio show. Meteorologists, who divide clouds into nine classes and subclasses, should also receive recognition since cumulonimbus clouds often reach altitudes exceeding forty thousand feet and receive the highest, i.e., **cloud nine** designation.

WOULDN'T TOUCH IT WITH A TEN-FOOT POLE: Before American railroads came into their own, travelers relied on primitive roads and a relatively advanced canal network. Power for water transport was supplied by mules on towpaths and humans wielding ten foot poles. The standard ten foot pole length was not arrived at arbitrarily; it resulted from careful calculations involving pole weight, waterway depths, and average distance to canal banks. Supplementing their standard functions, ten foot poles also pushed away unpleasant or dangerous obstacles, from whence came **wouldn't touch it with a ten-foot pole** as our national expression of revulsion.

ELEVENTH HOUR: The eleventh hour may be found in Matthew 20:1:16 and, because menial labor was performed from dawn to dusk, refers to the last hour of sunlight rather than the hour before midnight. Jesus' message proclaimed that the kingdom of heaven was comparable to a vineyard which paid all workers, even those arriving at **the eleventh hour**, equal wages. The gist of Christ's unusual communiqué conveyed the comforting thought that, even at the last possible moment, sufficient time remains for worthy supplicants to enter the kingdom of heaven.

BAKER'S DOZEN: Numerous cultures throughout recorded history have enforced severe penalties against bakers selling underweight loaves of bread. In 1266 England's Parliament passed strict laws regarding this matter, even though bread baking technology was not sufficiently advanced to create loaves of uniform weight. Fear of unjust punishment motivated bakers to protect themselves by adding an additional or "vantage loaf" to every twelve delivered. Not only did weight discrepancy problems disappear, but we are occasionally blessed with the opportunity of purchasing thirteen items for the price of twelve.

On the Wagon
Falling off the Wagon
Three Sheets to the Wind
Loaded to the Gills
Suits to a T
Hair of the Dog

One consequence of England's industrial revolution was a rapid increase in the number of urban poor. This segment of society received virtually no education or social services, and a plentiful supply of cheap gin made matters even worse. Around 1750 the establishment responded to a rising tide of mob violence by passing laws making even the smallest crime a capital offense. Little was accomplished with these measures except for the creation of a large death row population that was periodically placed on display as a tourist attraction.

Wagons were used to transport prisoners to places of execution, and before long, one last pub stop became customary. Sometimes regular patrons offered to buy a second round, a humanitarian gesture the guards usually turned down because the condemned were **on the wagon**. Britain's repressive laws have long since been repealed, but individuals attempting to abstain continue their precarious journey **on the wagon**. Conversely, those unable to resist temptation tend to be criticized for **falling off the wagon**.

Those exhibiting tendencies to **fall off the wagon** on a regular basis are often categorized by their peers as **three sheets to the wind** or **loaded to the gills**. In the nautical world, sheets refer to ropes used to reign in or extend sails. Losing simultaneous control of a vessel's sheets results in an inability to navigate and poses hazards for all on board. Describing dangerously drunk individuals as **three sheets to the wind** therefore **suits to a T**, meaning that this designation is just as perfect as the right angle on a draftsman's T square.

Fish and humans both possess gills, except that ours refer to the fleshy area under our jaws. **Loaded to the gills** thus accurately describes the state of excessive imbibers after their alcoholic consumption has theoretically filled all body cavities from foot to neck.

Hair of the dog that bit you was once considered an antidote for such bites. While modern medicine has discarded that notion, doctors have been known to prescribe supplemental doses of alcohol to alleviate the lingering effects of hangovers. Accordingly, **hair of the dog** is often suggested as a cure to those whose immoderate behavior has left them in dire straits.

Don't Let Them Get Your Goat
Getting Your Dander Up
Seeing Red
Moment of Truth
Venting Your Spleen
Raising One's Hackles
Keep Your Shirt On

The breeding and racing of horses has been one of mankind's abiding passions for thousands of years. Over the centuries this activity evolved into a world wide business requiring large amounts of capital, as well as the courage to assume enormous risks.

Throughout the years various breeding techniques produced many superior but high strung, hard to handle animals. Early on, however, someone discovered that tethering goats with horses created soothing effects which prevented skittish horses from injuring themselves. The calming influence provided by these companions was so powerful, and their sudden removal created such severe reactions, that goat stealing became rampant whenever major racing events drew near. As a result we have taken to offering those plagued by the inconsiderate actions of others the advice of **don't let them get your goat**.

Webster defines dander as "anger." Dander was actually a catalyst once used in the West Indies for speeding up the fermentation process in the production of molasses from sugar. **Getting your dander up** thus indicates that you have worked yourself into a state of anger or ferment which, if not reined in, will allow your tormentors to **get your goat**.

Bull fighting specializes in goading harassed, color blind bulls into charging repeatedly at red or brightly colored capes and was introduced to Spain by the Moors around A.D. 1000. Even though the unfortunate animals are chasing movement rather than color, sudden surges of anger seldom fail to deter us from **seeing red**. We are likewise indebted to both matador and bull for providing us with the **moment of truth**, or the critical point in time when a coup de grace must be administered both gracefully and accurately.

Should none of the above suffice for the purpose of **venting your spleen**, an organ once thought to harbor malicious feelings, you might voice the opinion that other people's irresponsible acts tend to **raise your hackles**. Apparently hackles, which are rooster or peacock neck feathers, rise dramatically whenever these birds become unduly agitated.

Shirts worn by gentlemen in the nineteenth century contained so much starch that indulging in strenuous activity was impossible while wearing these uncomfortable garments. Ever since, those of us aiming to avoid physical confrontations with potential trouble makers have attempted to diffuse the issue at hand with the admonition to **keep your shirt on**.

White Elephant
There's a Sucker Born Every Minute
Never Give a Sucker an Even Break

Anything we don't wish to own but can't get rid of tends to be called a **white elephant**. In ancient Siam albino elephants automatically became the property of the king, received the best of care and, because of their special status, were not allowed to work. Wealthy citizens unfortunate enough to incur the displeasure of their monarch were sometimes punished with the gift of a **white elephant**. Financial ruin inevitably followed as these beasts had ferocious appetites and provided nothing in return.

American showman P.T. Barnum further enhanced this concept of undesirability. When another circus acquired a rare albino specimen, Barnum promptly whitewashed his entire herd and hoped it wouldn't rain. A major advertising campaign soon convinced the gullible public that white was commonplace, turning his competitor's genuine article into an instant liability.

The obscure origins of **there's a sucker born every minute** and **never give a sucker an even break** are often erroneously attributed to P.T. Barnum. This error is understandable since Barnum's fondness for duplicity was so colossal that he even surcharged patrons to see the "egress." Many a country bumpkin eagerly pressed on to experience this marvel, only to find himself back on the street.

Some years ago the People's Republic of China attempted to market a new camera in the United States. Sales were dismal despite intensive advertising and excellent product quality. It seems our nation does not have a monopoly on cultural mistakes. The trademark of China's new offering was, you guessed it, **the white elephant**.

Hooker
Hunky-Dory
Red Light District
Painting the Town Red

General Joseph Hooker was born in 1814 and, after graduating from West Point, provided distinguished service in several campaigns including the Mexican War. In 1853 this promising officer left the army in order to manage a farm he had purchased near Sonoma, California.

The outbreak of our Civil War motivated "Fighting Joe," a nickname subsequently acquired during this conflict, to offer his services to the Union cause. Hooker quickly achieved the reputation of an extremely dependable commander who constantly voiced great concern for the lives and comfort of his men. Accordingly, camp followers were not discouraged, and women providing certain services for the troops came to be called **Hooker's girls**. A lack of political acumen caused the general's career to end in obscurity, but his name will forever remain associated with practitioners of the world's oldest profession.

At times we get tired of saying "O.K." and might be tempted to venture that everything's **hunky-dory**. Few people realize that **hunky-dory** refers to the English translation of a certain street name located in Yokohama, Japan. Yokohama is a major port serving Tokyo, and crews from many nations consider this city to be their second home. Naturally, a wide range of amenities are available to this multitude of temporary citizens, including modern versions of **Hooker's girls** who ply their trade in **hunky-dory** street.

In addition to selling liquor, saloons in the American West discretely advertised other services by placing red lanterns in their windows. Since these establishments tended to congregate in well defined areas of any particular community, that section of town inevitably became the **red light district**. Moving herds of cattle from ranches to railheads was an exhausting, time consuming task that deprived cowboys of both alcohol and female companionship for months at a time.

At trail's end the release of pent-up energies, combined with the type of entertainment offered in **red light districts**, often exploded into wild parties during which participants **painted the town red**.

Two, Four, Six Bits
Not Worth a Continental
Not Worth a Plug Nickel
Not Worth a Red Cent

Trade during America's colonial period was dependent on a combination of barter and coinage, with tobacco constituting the most important medium of exchange. As the economy expanded, England ignored her colonies' hard currency requirements, allowing the void to be filled with a hodge podge of gold and silver coins from other nations. One of these coins was the Spanish milled dollar consisting of eight reals or "bits," equal to 12 $\frac{1}{2}$ cents each.

One of Congress's new powers granted by the 1781 Articles of Confederation concerned the regulation of our national coinage. New York lawyer Gouverneur Morris proposed a coinage reform based on units of $\frac{1}{1440}$ of a dollar for easy conversion to popular foreign coins. Luckily, no decision was reached until 1784, when Thomas Jefferson's idea of substituting the more logical decimal system prevailed. **Two bits** thus became a quarter while **four bits** and **six bits** equaled fifty and seventy-five cents respectively. Immortalized in song (shave and a haircut, two bits) and language (it's a two bit operation), the designation of a quarter as **two bits** has remained a part of our culture.

In 1775 thirteen colonies convened a Continental Congress in Philadelphia to supervise our first venture into the realm of self-government. Not surprisingly, a lack of both precious metal and tax collecting power made paper money authorized by Congress to pay for the revolution, **not worth a Continental**.

Alexander Hamilton became our first Secretary of the Treasury and proposed adding silver to our pennies to allow for a reduction in size. In 1792 an experimental cent was produced with a plug of silver in the middle, but no coins were stuck for circulation because the temptation to remove the plug would have been irresistible. The evolution of language is not always logical because we should really be saying that something is not worth a plug cent rather than **not worth a plug nickel**.

From 1798 to 1838 planchets used to strike our pennies were imported from England. These coins resembled English pennies in size and contained a high copper content, giving them a reddish appearance. Heavy and impractical, they were phased out in 1857 and replaced with a smaller, more useful coin.

Our legacy from these various economic and monetary experiments remains self-evident since we regularly use **not worth a Continental, not worth a plug nickel** or **not worth a red cent** when referring to objects or plans of so little value as to be beneath contempt.

Tell it to the Marines
Tell it to the Judge
Till the Cows Come Home

In 1664 H.M.S. *Defyance* returned from a voyage during which flying fish had been observed for the first time. The court of King James II absolutely refused to believe such a tall tale, and a lively argument ensued. Confirmation came from a visiting marine officer, creating an even greater ruckus. King James II had had enough and issued the following royal proclamation. "Our maritime officers are not only loyal and courageous, they are also keen observers of all that transpires on the seas. Henceforth, whenever a story of this nature comes our way, we will first **tell it to the marines.**"

Ships' officers and crew were immediately made aware of the King's wishes. Not surprisingly, the navy's ordinary seamen showed little interest in complying with this new directive but did expropriate its **tell it to the marines** portion for expressing cynical disbelief concerning any and all pronouncements issued by their superiors.

In later years the civilian equivalent of **tell it to the marines** became **tell it to the judge**. Law enforcement officers often exhort newly arrested suspects protesting their innocence to pipe down and **tell it to the judge**. A corollary usage of this expression involves youngsters convicted of misdemeanors who are offered a second chance after agreeing to **tell it to the judge**.

The proper course of action relating to the treatment of juvenile offenders has been argued to no avail **till the cows come home**. Cows, who have a way of their own, display a propensity for wandering home whenever the mood strikes them. Their tedious movement has therefore led to the adoption of **till the cows come home** as a popular figure of speech for the purpose of describing the snail-like progress of inconclusive, irresolvable arguments or discussions.

Charles Dickens

Although Charles Dickens never quite equaled William Shakespeare's prolific contribution to the English language, we are nevertheless indebted to the former for his probable invention and popularization of the following gems.

Bag of bones
Oliver Twist
Between you, me and the lamp post
Nicholas Nickelby
Dull as dishwater
Our Mutual Friend
Eat your hat
Pickwick Papers
Every man jack
Barnaby Rudge
Get a leg on
Pickwick Papers
Hard as nails
Oliver Twist
Last straw (that broke the camels back)
Dombey & Sons
Not what it's cracked up to be
Martin Chuzzlewitt
Put that in your pipe and smoke it
Pickwick Papers
Put the kibosh (kye-bosk) on
Seven Dials
Quick study
Nicholas Nickelby
The law is an ass
Oliver Twist
Wax angry
The Old Curiosity shop

Blitzkrieg
Quisling
Turncoat
The Jig is Up
Benedict Arnold
Fifth Column

Adolf Hitler's successful introduction of **blitzkrieg** or "lightning war" touched off World War II and plunged the world into its greatest conflagration of all time. Germany also failed to anticipate the difficulties she would face regarding the administration of so much newly acquired territory. Sad to say, Hitler's Third Reich ably solved this problem with the help of a few citizens from every newly subjugated nation who voluntarily turned against their own people. One such individual was a Norwegian army officer named Vidkun Quisling, who, because of Hitler's strong support, remained in control of a subservient Norwegian government throughout the war years.

So despised was Quisling that at war's end Norway changed her law against capital punishment for the express purpose of executing this **turncoat**. The name **Quisling** thus became a generic word for traitor, losing its capital Q in the process.

One can be more sympathetic to Benedict Arnold, a brilliant soldier who served the American Revolution with great skill and courage. Unfortunately, he quarreled with his superiors after being accused of inappropriate behavior, and, when George Washington himself reprimanded Arnold for living high on the hog, the latter decided to switch sides.

In 1780 Benedict Arnold wangled command of West Point in order to turn this important fortress over to the British. The plot failed when Major Andre, Arnold's English contact, was captured. Discovering just in the nick of time that **the jig was up** (jig was once English slang for "cheat" or "trick"), Benedict Arnold turned his highly visible coat inside out and slipped away to join the British in New York.

This historical episode unwittingly gave us **turncoat** and **Benedict Arnold** for describing citizens engaged in treasonous activities. Not surprisingly, history has treated Arnold with more compassion than Quisling because printed references to the former have not deleted the capital letters from his name.

The Spanish Civil War provides us with an additional synonym for traitorous activity. In 1937 Franco's army advanced on the city of Madrid from four directions using army units designated as "columns." At the same time, Franco sympathizers located within the beleaguered city created diversions, disorienting the defenders. This quasi-military force appropriated the name of Hemingway's popular novel **The Fifth Column**, a label that was subsequently applied to spies and saboteurs during World War II.

**The Coast is Clear
Bathtub Gin
Mickey Finn
The Real McCoy
Pussyfooting Around
Throwing the Book
Bootlegger**

America's eighteenth constitutional amendment, better known as the Volstead Act or "prohibition," was undoubtedly one of the most ill-conceived social experiments of all time. Passed in 1920, this legislation enticed hordes of previous non-drinkers to sample a now illegal commodity while, at the same time, providing a catalyst for turning insignificant criminal enterprises into economic powerhouses.

Trade in illicit "booze" became a huge, even socially acceptable, business with large volumes of liquor flowing in from Canada. Even greater quantities arrived from ships waiting patiently outside our territorial limits for signals from lookouts that **the coast was clear**. Product quality often left much to be desired, and when supplies were augmented with homemade **bathtub gin**, illness or blindness became distinct possibilities. Should a **Mickey Finn** be added to these concoctions, one's chances of suffering permanent damage escalated dramatically. Evidently a small time hoodlum named Mickey Finn immortalized his name in a previous generation by slipping knock-out potions into the drinks of potential robbery victims.

Bill McCoy, a resident of Nova Scotia and a boat builder by trade, possessed an unusual code of honor. Upon entering the lucrative business of **bootlegging**, he avoided entanglements with the underworld and sold only goods of the highest quality. Eventually McCoy ran afoul of the law, but, because of his high standards and outstanding reputation, we invariably certify goods and services of unquestioned quality as **the real McCoy**.

The concept of **pussyfooting around**, a synonym for imitating elegant, stealthy feline movements, became popular during the same era. Prohibition advocates were nicknamed **pussyfooters** in honor of their hero, "Pussyfoot" Eugene Williams, an ardent prohibitionist famous for his sneaky law enforcement tactics.

During the tumultuous 1920s and 1930s judges started **throwing the book** at convicted **bootleggers** and gangsters. This figure of speech for imposing the maximum sentence allowed by law is not only graphic but also satisfies our instinctive yearning for law and order.

Mr. McCoy and his compatriots inherited the colorful nickname of **bootlegger** from eighteenth century seamen, whose long leather boots stretched from toe to thigh and turned out to be ideal for smuggling all manner of contraband.

The Right
The Left
Middle of the Road
Let Them Eat Cake

In the 1680's Louis XIV decided to govern France from Ver-sailles, a small community located just outside of Paris. France's nobles were required to accompany the "Sun King" to this backwater where he successfully monitored their activities; hatching of plots was thwarted, and successive monarchs managed to retain both their crowns and heads for the next one hundred years.

The French revolution ended this idyllic arrangement, and by 1789 France's government consisted of a constitutional monarch, a president, and two legislative bodies made up of nobles and commoners. Despite all the rhetoric and new ideals, a certain amount of suspicion and mistrust accompanied such a major change. Thinking perhaps of Louis XIV, the nobles were corralled in an area whose seats happened to be on the president's right, leaving the commoners little choice except to arrange themselves on the opposite or left side.

Nobles favored preserving the status quo and clung to traditional points of view, whereas commoners sought to change their condition and espoused more liberal philosophies. The use of the words **right** and **left** of center thus became equated with the leanings of these two groups. At the time few paved roads existed past city limits, and only those traveling in the road's middle could expect to make any progress. As the French political process matured, a widening chasm emerged between the **right** and the **left**, forcing **middle of the road** compromises in order to resolve an endless series of controversial issues.

History provides many instances wherein the ruling classes' inability or unwillingness to recognize and redress grievances ultimately led to revolution. The French experience towards the end of the 18th century produced such an example. After governmental mismanagement reduced the country's standard of living to a point of desperation, Marie Antionette responded with her infamous reply of "If there isn't any bread, **let them eat cake**." Since that time this unusually callous quotation has been repeated by other authorities in its condensed form of **let them eat cake** on occasions when their own inadequacies had to be glossed over or explained away. In the long run, the establishment's disregard of the people's plight proved to be fatal. Although Marie Antionette and Louis XVI escaped the revolution's initial impact, a continuing reign of terror eventually sent them, along with thousands of other victims, to the guillotine.

Maverick
Marching to the Tune of a Different Drummer
Earmark

In 1803, the year of Samuel Augustus Maverick's birth, Texas was a large, borderless, sparsely inhabited Mexican province struggling to contain an infiltration of land-seeking adventurers from the eastern United States. Thirty years later, Maverick was destined to both fight for and sign the Texas Declaration of Independence, after which he settled into the practice of law and indulged in periodic land speculation. Contrary to some accounts, Maverick was not a rancher and was basically uninterested in acquiring either cattle or grazing land.

On one occasion, Maverick did accept four hundred head of cattle to settle a real estate debt, turning them over to an old family retainer for management purposes. Unfortunately, Maverick's employee possessed neither knowledge nor enthusiasm concerning the care and feeding of livestock and evaded his responsibilities by setting them free to roam the open range. Unattended, they nevertheless survived and multiplied, although there is no record of their ultimate fate. Serious ranchers operating in the same area distinguished their branded cattle from this influx of unmarked animals by calling the latter **mavericks**. Since the untrammeled **mavericks** wandered about as they pleased, society has decided to classify as **mavericks** all men or beasts who prefer **marching to the tune of a different drummer**.

Curiously enough, Sam Maverick provided us with a descendent named Maury Maverick who became a congressman in the 1930s. This gentlemen turned out to be a **maverick** in more than just name as no one, from the president on down, ever managed to influence his vote.

Ranchers in the American West did not invent the concept of marking livestock for identification purposes. Throughout the ages, animal's ears have been cut or notched in specific patterns in order to record ownership. This ancient practice of earmarking therefore lets us **earmark**, i.e. identify and segregate, funds or physical objects for timely distribution at some later date.

Dutch Courage
The Admiral's Broom
Going Dutch
Dutch Treat
Getting in Dutch
Dutch Uncle
Dutch Defense
Double Dutch
Dutch Act
Dutch Reckoning
Dutch Talent

Throughout the 1652-53 Anglo-Dutch naval war, England was forced to endure destructive raids reaching far up the Thames estuary. The spectacle of little Holland twisting the mighty lion's tail proved to be most humiliating, motivating Great Britain to shove her propaganda machine into high gear.

Rumors soon circulated to the effect that Dutch sailors were cowardly and unwilling to fight until large quantities of Dutch gin had been consumed. Even though these allegations turned out to be unfounded, the words **Dutch courage** became standard fare for describing situations requiring alcoholic fortification.

No clear victory emerged from this conflict except that Dutch seamen were clearly vindicated after winning the battle of Dungeness. With a broom secured on high Admiral Van Tromp roamed the channel at will, showing the world that England had been swept from the seas. In future wars ships returning to port signaled successfully completed missions by displaying brooms in similar positions, continuing a naval tradition that has been handed down to us as **the admiral's broom**.

German immigrants settling in Pennsylvania were nicknamed the "Pennsylvania Dutch" because the word for German in that language is "Deutsch." Other Americans, vaguely aware that the Dutch had been among our earliest settlers, easily confused both these cultures and words. Our new German-American citizens exhibited a strong work ethic, brought up their children strictly, and did not believe in spending money frivolously. Their culture thus gave us the legacy of **going Dutch** or **Dutch treat**, meaning that each party pays his own way, and **getting in Dutch** which is reserved for children who misbehave and get caught.

Dutch uncle refers to well meaning, bumbling relatives dispensing unsolicited advice, an image hardly befitting the Pennsylvania Dutch stereotype. Even more mysterious are the origins of **Dutch defense** (surrender), **Double Dutch** (misleading conversation), **Dutch act** (suicide), **Dutch reckoning** (poor navigation) and **Dutch talent** (strong back-weak mind). One can readily understand why, in 1934, the Dutch government showed its displeasure with this disparaging language by promoting the substitution of "Netherlands" for "Dutch" wherever possible.

Frog
Limey
Gringo
Yankee

Frenchmen are sometimes called **Frogs** because in France the legs of these little amphibians have long been accorded the status of a national delicacy. This has not always been as obvious as it seems today. After our revolutionary conflict with Great Britain drew to a close, Washington's officers decided to host a farewell dinner party for their French allies. The Americans were vaguely aware of their guests' partiality to frogs but lacked specific information, and the language barrier forestalled any constructive consultation. By dinner time the frog problem remained unresolved so that the cook, relying on **Yankee** ingenuity, handed the ranking American officer a very large live bullfrog which he ceremoniously swished around in his soup. The French watched this spectacle in silent astonishment, concluding it was some sort of quaint colonial custom. They became even more perturbed after our junior officers repeated the process and passed the frog across the table, giving their French counterparts little choice but to follow suit.

In the mid-eighteenth century British surgeon James Lind published a widely read paper on scurvy. While serving in the Royal Navy, Lind had been appalled by the incidence of scurvy which caused rotten gums, loss of teeth, and general debilitation. After studying the men's inadequate diet, he predicted that adding citrus fruit would completely eliminate this scourge. Even though Lind's theory was soon proven correct, forty years passed before limes became standard issue on all British men of war. As this knowledge spread throughout the world's navies, American sailors started calling their British counterparts **Limeys**. Used initially only in military circles the **limey** moniker came, in due time, to include the entire English population.

Gringo first appeared in a Madrid newspaper around 1780 as a disparaging name for those who had not acquired a true Castillian accent. The new word seemed to possess just the right amount of derogatory connotation, and when North Americans started meddling south of the border, the natives began classifying these unwelcome intruders as **Gringos**.

Peter Stuyvesant became colonial governor of New Amsterdam in 1647 and, sensing a vulnerability to British attack, built his famous wooden wall guarding the town's northern border. Stuyvesant's worst fears were realized in 1664 when four British frigates sailed up the harbor, ignored all defensive preparations, and forced the city's surrender without firing a shot. New Amsterdam was renamed New York in honor of King Charles II's brother, the Duke of York. England's new subjects were immediately saddled with the derisive nickname of "John cheese" or "Jan kaas" in Dutch. Jan kaas mutated into **Yankees**, a name that in due time spread to include all northern colonial residents. Expansion continued unabated and by the 1860s all citizens who remained loyal to the Union and lived east of the Mississippi River joined the **Yankee** category.

Buying a Pig in a Poke
Letting the Cat Out of the Bag
Skeleton in the Closet
Bringing Home the Bacon
Living High on the Hog
Kicking the Bucket
Croak

Traveling country fairs in Medieval England provided opportunities for trade, created highly valued social contacts, and lasted anywhere from a few days to several weeks depending on the community's wealth and importance. Participating merchants offered a variety of products, although not all transactions were consummated in a honorable manner. Dishonest vendors sometimes tied a cat in a sack or "poke," claiming to be offering a fat young pig, while prospective buyers were denied inspection privileges on the grounds that the animal might escape. Many a naive yokel fell for this trick, paying good money and returning home only to find himself the proud owner of a mangy alley cat. Ever since, acquiring goods sight unseen or accepting pronouncements at face value has translated into **buying a pig in a poke**.

Sophisticated citizens who insisted on viewing before paying not only **let the cat out of the bag** but, if they had lived in the 1800s, might also have unmasked a **skeleton in the closet**. In the nineteenth century doctors striving to increase their anatomical knowledge by dissecting cadavers ran the risk of both public outrage and accusations of ghoulish behavior. Their experiments were, of necessity, conducted in secret, with skeletal remains ending up in dark corners or closets. Once the general public became aware of these activities they began commenting on skeletons presumed to be secreted in their doctors' closets. Physicians eventually managed to rid themselves of this social stigma, while the rest of us learned from painful experience that our personal **skeletons in the closet** should be kept well hidden from public view.

Pigs play an important role in the world economy and individuals managing to augment the family inventory of these animals have always been held in high esteem for **bringing home the bacon**, an activity we now honor in a monetary sense as well.

Hogs provide us with an incredible variety of products. The best cuts such as ham, pork chops, tenderloin, spare ribs, and bacon are found high up on the pig's side, an anatomical anomaly allowing financially secure families to **live high on the hog**.

Before these goodies find their way to our tables, the inevitable slaughtering process must take place. At one time this was accomplished by hanging the unfortunate creatures on metal frames or "buckets." In their death throes, hogs kicked and banged against the sides of this equipment, providing us with **kicking the bucket** as an unusually graphic synonym for our departure from this world.

Usage of **kicking the bucket** must share the limelight with **croak**, which supposedly likens our last gasps to the croaking of frogs. One must take this particular colloquialism with a grain of salt, since noises emanating from expiring humans could never even begin to duplicate the infinite variety of sounds provided for our enjoyment by the species Rana.

Philadelphia Lawyer
Railroaded

Should we knowingly find ourselves on the wrong side of the law, the temptation arises to look for a **Philadelphia lawyer**. This means we are seeking the services of someone noted for his or her ability to win lost causes by obscuring the issue at hand through the use of impassioned and devious oratory.

In 1735 Peter Zenger, publisher of the *New York City Weekly Journal*, was charged with libel for exposing corruption in the New York colonial governor's office. Under British rule, freedom of the press as we know it today did not exist. In fact the establishment's authority was so complete that telling the truth was not considered an adequate defense against a libel charge.

No local attorney dared to defend Zenger, but a wider search produced a courageous lawyer from Philadelphia named Andrew Hamilton. Mr. Hamilton's arguments were so persuasive that the defendant was acquitted despite the very clear language of the law. Not only was Mr. Zenger afforded the opportunity to continue practicing his chosen profession, but the concept of freedom of the press in America was born.

Such a radical idea did not gain currency overnight and, because existing law had indeed been circumvented, inhabitants of the various colonies started making jokes about **Philadelphia lawyers**. We still use the shortened version of one favorite quote counseling that "if you are innocent pray to God, but if guilty find yourself a **Philadelphia lawyer**."

Unsophisticated wrongdoers failing to secure the services of a **Philadelphia lawyer** often find themselves **railroaded**, our equivalent word for speedy trials ending in guilty verdicts. **Railroading** is a term left over from the days when hastily constructed railroads first connected the far-flung reaches of our continent. At the time private resources were unequal to the task at hand, causing the U.S. Government to offer public land subsidies for every mile of track laid. Construction speed thus became all important, and railroad projects charged ahead at full throttle, in the process of which the rights of native American tribes were often disregarded. Knotty problems were left behind for future generations to ponder, while investors gained title to large tracts of valuable land through the practice of **railroading**.

Cooling Our Heels
Long in the Tooth
Wet Behind the Ears
Don't Look a Gift Horse in the Mouth
Straight from the Horse's Mouth
Don't Change Horses in Midstream
Horse Sense

An estimated 80 percent of the population tilled the soil throughout North America's early colonial period just to feed themselves and provide sustenance for those engaged in other professions. Since farming was the only viable occupation for most citizens, prime land, livestock, and equipment were all categorized as precious commodities. Young farmers relied heavily on relatives for the acquisition of these basic necessities, and next to land, horses were probably the most significant contribution one could receive.

Horses provided both farm labor and long-distance, high-speed transportation. Overheating and sore legs were averted through mandatory rest periods, allowing one's mount to **cool its heels**. Riders tended to chafe over the necessary delays, and we voice our displeasure as well upon being subjugated to arbitrary periods of inactivity or waiting that obligate us to **cool our heels**.

Foals are born with small, straight teeth that do not make contact with each other. As the maturing process unfolds, these teeth grow larger, come together, and move slightly outward to facilitate chewing and grazing. In later years horse's gums recede, providing an impression of even longer teeth. Consequently, **long in the tooth** has come to identify those whose advanced age is under discussion.

Professionals in all fields of endeavor tend to explain failure on the part of over-anxious neophytes by proclaiming that they're still **wet behind the ears**. Foals, as well as many other animals, arrive in this world covered with womb liquids. Indentations behind the ears invariably take the longest to dry out, a natural phenomena which endows us with one more expressive colloquialism.

A horse's approximate age can be determined by examining its mouth. Except for livestock transactions, it has always been considered impolite to apply this knowledge for the purpose of determining remaining years of useful life. Properly brought up children therefore **did not look a gift horse in the mouth**. Although horses play minor roles in our present world, the social message remains unchanged: one does not publicly question the value of any gift.

Horses have enriched our language even further. Upon divulging inside information we tend to emphasize our claim for accuracy by saying it's **straight from the horse's mouth. Don't change horses in mid-stream** was presented to the American electorate by Abraham Lincoln, who offered this sage advice in his 1864 presidential nomination acceptance speech. Friends contemplating major and perhaps risky changes are similarly charged, while disasters resulting from ignoring this prudent advice are often attributed to a lack of **horse sense**.

It's a Lead Pipe Cinch
Playing a Hunch
Make No Bones About It
Boning Up

Ancient cultures were totally unaware of lead's inherent health hazards and used this material to line the bottoms of both drinking vessels and storage containers. Only the wealthy could afford these luxuries, leading historical researchers to give serious consideration to the theory that lead's toxicity may have contributed to the unstable mental state exhibited by so many of those entrusted with political power. Until fairly recently, lead-based products could be found in abundance throughout our own homes as well. Lead pipes were cheaper than galvanized iron or copper, could be bent to almost any shape without losing integrity, and produced dependable plumbing systems.

In the early 1900s horses still constituted a preferred form of transport and saddles were attached to these beasts of burden by means of leather straps or "cinches." Searching for words to describe an unalterable set of circumstances must have led someone with a vivid imagination to envision a combination of dependable lead pipes and securely fastened leather straps. This mental exercise undoubtedly produced **it's a lead pipe cinch** for emphasizing one's opinion that the occurrence or successful conclusion of any particular event is completely beyond question.

Naturally not everything is **a lead pipe cinch**, forcing us to use our intuition when making educated guesses. We call this process **playing a hunch** proving, whether we realize it or not, that mankind instinctively clings to past superstitions. In medieval times it was considered a sure sign of good fortune to touch a hunchback's hump, a myth we perpetuate every time one of us **plays a hunch**.

Some investors love to **play hunches**, while others **make no bones about it** that **boning up** on one's subject matter constitutes a less speculative approach. Years ago establishments catering to the less affluent served soup containing bone fragments. The upper classes could, however, claim with both conviction and accuracy that their soup would arrive bone free. In other words they **made no bones about it** and neither do we when it comes to altering our firmly held opinions.

African cultures developed the notion that future events were predictable by studying the configuration of bones tossed into a ring. Slaves living in the New World preserved this ritual, referring to the custom as **boning up**. Today's serious student now spends inordinate amounts of time **boning up** for exams, although he or she is seeking knowledge rather than an opportunity to dabble in the occult.

O.K.

O.K. has managed to transcend innumerable language and cultural barriers, becoming one of the most universally used expressions of all time. Some believe it evolved from African cultures brought to the new world by slaves. Others favor the theory that when French ships entered New Orleans they were cleared "au quai," meaning "to the dock" but pronounced **O.K.** The most plausible origin of all, however, stems from one particular family of Hudson valley settlers.

The ancient Greeks not only knew that the world was round but also managed a surprisingly accurate assessment of its circumference. Most fifteenth century scientists agreed with the Greek calculations and advised their monarchs that western routes to China were impractical. Columbus disagreed, believing a relatively short voyage would meet his objectives. Columbus lucked out by discovering previously unknown lands, although subsequent explorers soon realized that his discoveries were not even remotely connected to the Asian mainland. Many optimists, however, remained firmly convinced that whatever barriers stood between them and the riches of the Orient amounted to no more than temporary inconveniences.

Renewed exploration efforts therefore focused on finding a water route through this new, supposedly narrow land mass known as the "New World." One early attempt was made by Henry Hudson, an English explorer working for the Dutch East India Company. In 1609 Hudson confidently sailed up the waterway destined to bear his name but soon realized that his quest was to be in vain. Twenty five miles south of present day Albany, Hudson observed some native American children playing near a bend in the river and named the area "Kinder Hoek," or children's corner in Dutch. Over the years a prosperous farming community grew up on this site bearing the now Anglicized name of Kinderhook.

Martin Van Buren, a descendant of early Dutch settlers, was born there in 1782. He became a leading citizen and was nicknamed "Old Kinderhook" because of his influence regarding local affairs. In 1836 Van Buren became the eighth president of the

United States, having served as governor of New York State prior to that time. In those days life was less complicated, and local citizens often traveled to Albany for the purpose of obtaining "Old Kinderhook's" help, signature, or perhaps just his initials on a document. Eventually the description of this procedure was shortened to getting the **O.K.**, a term now used throughout the entire world for obtaining permission or describing a satisfactory situation.

Turning a Blind Eye
Maginot Line Mentality

Horatio Nelson was probably Great Britain's greatest naval hero. Two separate campaigns cost Nelson the loss of an eye and an arm, providing living proof that his victories were not won without great personal sacrifice. In April of 1801, Nelson's squadron of shallow draft vessels was sent close to the Danish coast for what history records as the Battle of Copenhagen, while Nelson's commanding officer, Sir Hyde Parker, remained at some distance on his flagship. As the battle progressed, it appeared to Admiral Parker that a stalemate was developing, and Nelson was sent a flag signal ordering him to disengage.

At that precise moment, the latter sensed a lessening of resolve on the Danish side. Placing a telescope to his blind eye, Nelson declared there was no signal to be seen and pressed on. His decision turned out to be correct, allowing an act of gross insubordination to be conveniently forgotten. This incident not only augmented Nelson's fame but also enriched our language by endowing us with the ability to **turn a blind eye** towards that which we choose not to see.

Accusing anyone of **turning a blind eye** is rather uncomplimentary. Expressing the belief that someone suffers from a **Maginot line mentality** is even worse. Andre' Maginot was France's Minister of War from 1929 to 1932 and thought only in terms of World War I's static lines when he built a series of impregnable forts on the French-German border. Maginot was not alone in failing to recognize Germany's advances in the use of air power and mobile infantry. Because France's general staff suffered from the same myopia, the huge French army hunkered down in its mammoth underground fortresses and waited patiently for Hitler to go away. Disaster struck in the form of mechanized infantry divisions supported by coordinated air attacks which charged through Belgium, outflanking a suddenly obsolete Maginot line.

Preparing for a future war based solely on experiences garnered from the previous one was instrumental in creating the Maginot Line debacle. At least a new colloquialism emerged from this painful lesson, allowing us to criticize those refusing to factor new evidence into current thinking as embracing a **Maginot Line mentality**.

Hoist With His Own Petard
Under the Gun
Loose Cannon
Bull in a China Shop

Although gunpowder was invented in China thousands of years ago, its secret formula did not reach the western world until around A.D.1200. Another hundred years passed before cannon barrel technology became reliable enough to provide the world's armies with their first weapons of mass destruction. Artillery could now reduce any fortification to rubble, even though the process was often both tedious and time consuming.

Research efforts to develop methods for hastening the destruction process led French engineers to invent a device they christened a "petard." This new piece of military hardware consisted of an oddly shaped keg packed with powder and equipped with a slow-burning fuse. Simple and effective, petards were attached to gates or walls under cover of darkness. Deployment of these crude time bombs became a hazardous occupation for sappers who were frequently **hoist with their own petard** due to premature explosions caused by unreliable fuses. Shakespeare's Hamlet mentions plotters **hoist with their own petard**, and other authors also preserved this unusual phrase for posterity by similarly describing the fate of those whose well laid plans somehow went awry.

The arms race is not a new phenomena. As cannon became more powerful, bastions guarding harbor entrances acquired bigger guns of their own. Ships attempting to slip into port undetected thus found themselves **under the gun**, a feeling we have all experienced when pressured into accomplishing complicated tasks within limited time frames.

Ship's cannon likewise kept pace with technological advances, evolving into heavy monsters requiring complicated rope and pulley operating systems. Enemy action or excessive wear often caused equipment failure, and the ensuing carnage resulting from a heaving ship with a loose cannon could be awesome. Humans lacking sensitivity to delicate situations are reminiscent of **loose cannon**, and their damage-inflicting capability has been likened to that of a **bull in a china shop**.

For centuries the destruction one might expect from free-roaming bulls in china shops has been effectively used as a metaphor. To settle a bet, New York's Plumbers China Shop once allowed actor Paul Douglas to lead a bull through the premises—on the condition that band leader Fred Waring provide compensation for any destroyed merchandise. The concept of automatic damage lost some of its luster as the bull's behavior turned out to be a model of propriety, while Paul Douglas nervously knocked over several displays.

Boardroom
Member of the Board
Chairman of the Board
Blue Collar
White Collar
Sacked
Fired
Golden Parachute

During the last quarter century, America's industries have struggled valiantly to maintain their technological supremacy in the face of overwhelming foreign competition. Despite the uncertainties involved, posh boardrooms and high CEO compensations have nevertheless managed to continue their existence as facts of life in corporate America.

Two hundred years ago our humble beginnings dictated quite a different set of circumstances. Large tables were equated with symbols of unattainable luxury, and corporate executives drew down modest salaries. Meeting room furniture often consisted of planks laid across sawhorses, plus one chair reserved for an important personage or "chairman." As wealth and furniture increased "board" was substituted for "plank," bequeathing us a legacy of **boardroom**, **member of the board**, and last but not least, **chairman of the board**.

Whenever the economy found itself on an upward path our fledgling corporations hired additional **blue collar** factory workers and **white collar** office employees, so named after each group's preferred shirt color. Unfortunately, periodic economic slumps also imposed the necessity of **sacking** or **firing** a portion of the work force.

In medieval days, craftsmen realized they had been **sacked** when their employer wordlessly handed them their own personal sack of tools. **Sacked** is not often used today, and hourly workers are "laid off" or "furloughed" rather than **fired**. In recent years a spate of corporate restructuring has resulted in offers of early retirement for middle management and irresistible **golden parachutes** for the top dogs.

Researching the origin of **fired** brought to light the story of a highly regarded employee finding himself dismissed by a major corporation under controversial circumstances. It appears the individual in question became so incensed over his perception of unfair treatment, that he incinerated or **fired** his desk. Whether or not this dramatic act granted a stay of execution remains unknown. We can only theorize that his extreme form of protest was sufficiently well remembered to create one more word for Mr. Webster's dictionary.

Learning the Ropes
Pipe Down
The Bitter End
Last Ditch Stand

Throughout the centuries, sailing ships evolved from a few basic types of hulls, sails and ropes to incredibly complex technological marvels. Typically, they reached their height of development and sophistication just as steamboats became economically viable alternatives.

Large ships required miles of rope divided into numerous subdivisions, each with their own name and function. An almost identical thickness and appearance of these segments only added to the confusion. Some lines could be identified only by the location of their deck-securing systems, making it very difficult for novice seamen to master their trade. Eventually some standardization evolved, providing relief to youngsters **learning their ropes**. The need for these skills are long gone but the importance of **learning the ropes** remains a constant, continuing factor throughout our every day life.

Commands used in the management of these complicated vessels had to be conveyed to crewmen in a clear and audible manner. This task was accomplished with a bosun's whistle or "pipe," which produced sounds for initiating every imaginable function. There was even a command for piping gatherings of loud, raucous men below deck. Since then all parents in the English-speaking world have on more than one occasion admonished their boisterous children to **pipe down**.

One set of notes from the pipe concerned an important piece of deck equipment called a "bit," whose function was to pay out mooring hawsers and anchor chains. Each of these lines was known as a "bitter" and its end, which remained attached to the bit, became **the bitter end**. Should the entire bitter be in the ocean without the anchor having found bottom, prudence dictated informing the captain they were at **the bitter end**.

Usage of **the bitter end** has expanded far beyond our nautical world. More than once, final messages from failing military campaigns have indicated that **the bitter end** was in sight and staving off complete annihilation depended on the success of a **last**

ditch stand.

In the eighteenth century, Bishop Gilbert Burnet published memoirs referring to the "last ditch" on a battlefield. This indicates there is no mystery or hidden meaning in the origin of **last ditch stand**, which can be employed in either a military or figurative mode.

Climbing on the Bandwagon
Dark Horse Candidate
Throwing One's Hat into the Ring

Nineteenth century small-town America possessed very limited means of communication, a problem that was partially solved by circulating the town band through the streets in a horse-drawn wagon. Their musical renditions invariably attracted nearby residents, enabling town officials to make announcements and dispense noteworthy news. Candidates for political office soon realized that riding along on this conveyance afforded maximum exposure while expending minimum physical effort. More importantly, each stop guaranteed the presence of a captive audience.

Citizens swayed by any specific candidate's oratory often indicated agreement by **climbing on the bandwagon**. At times this act generated chain reactions of additional support, the length of which was limited only by the horse's endurance!

In those days national conventions were not placid affairs, and sometimes numerous ballots were suffered before a presidential choice emerged. During this tedious procedure, a rising tide of support sometimes suddenly swung towards one particular candidate, causing undecided delegates, fearful of losing out on subsequently dispensed favors, to **climb on the bandwagon**.

Sometimes circumstances produced stubborn deadlocks resolvable only by allowing enigmatic personalities to capture their party's nomination. Individuals thus selected came to be called **dark horse candidates**, so named because of their swift rise from total obscurity. This interesting phraseology survived the passage of time, and we often hear politicians discussing potential **dark horse candidates** whenever convention time draws near.

Ambitious individuals by-passed as **dark horse candidates** might nevertheless announce availability by **throwing their hats into the ring**. This expression came from the time when John Sullivan reigned as heavyweight boxing champion of the world. In a quest for additional publicity, Sullivan promised prize money to anyone lasting in the ring with him for a specified number of rounds. Occasionally a few brave challengers signaled their desire to participate by actually **throwing their hats into the ring**. While few of these intrepid souls lasted long enough to make any money, their efforts did at least provide us with one more lasting contribution to our political language.

Bulls & Bears
Keep It Under Your Hat
Watered Stock
Blue Chip Stocks
Bucket Shops
Blue-Sky Laws
Cornering the Market

The London Stock Exchange was organized in 1773 and has grown into one of the world's foremost financial institutions. Initially most of its listed securities consisted of government bonds whose prices tended to fluctuate quite widely. Investors who thought a major decline was due would sell short and were accused of "bearing down" on the market. Others, who were somewhat less pessimistic, might just sell securities already owned, after which they were bare (also spelled beare) of stocks. Not illogically, those with negative points of view became known as bears. Buyers of securities now required a label as well, and since organized fights between bulls and bears constituted a popular pastime, an irresistible play on words led optimists to become **bulls.**

Coincidentally, the perceived nature of these two animals is very well suited to stock market gyrations because bears convey an image of growling and retreating, whereas bulls are known for their propensity to charge ahead regardless of risk.

A plaque near today's 60 Wall Street commemorates a 1792 meeting held under a sycamore tree involving three brokerage firms and twenty-one individuals. Rules of conduct and commission rates were agreed upon, laying the foundations for an organization that eventually became the New York Stock Exchange. One rule provided that securities sold must be transferred to buyers by the next business day. Brokers could thus be seen walking up and down Wall Street delivering certificates they had carefully concealed in their tall top hats. Although today's brokers transfer securities electronically they, along with the rest of us, continue to be charged with the responsibility of keeping confidential information **under our hats.**

One of Wall Street's traditional functions consists of raising venture capital through the sale of common stock. During periods of speculative excess, new issues often wend their way to market at inflated prices, a practice known as selling **watered stock**. This lovely phrase came from our western cattle drives where cows, or "stock," were fed prodigious quantities of first salt and then water just prior to being weighed and sold.

Savvy investors avoid **watered stock** in favor of **blue chip stocks**, an honor accorded to only a few hundred of our most highly regarded publicly traded companies. The idea of categorizing certain securities as **blue chips** came from the game of poker, in which red chips represent the lowest values while **blue chips** weigh in at amounts up to ten times as high.

Unsophisticated security purchasers tend to be cheated by **bucket shop** operators promoting questionable investments. At one time **bucket shops** referred to saloons where cheap beer was available by the bucket. This name arrived on our financial scene after the Chicago Board of Trade instituted requirements banning grain trades of less than five thousands bushels. Illegal small-lot trading continued anyway, with those engaged in this activity buying "buckets" of grain from **bucket shops.**

In 1912 Kansas became the first of many states to enact laws protecting the public against fraudulent investment schemes. Press coverage implied that these new regulations would forevermore ban con-artists from selling everything, including the blue sky, to unwary speculators. Publicity generated by this landmark legislation picked up on the "blue sky" reference, and ever since, issuers of new securities have had to comply with each individual state's **blue-sky laws.**

Cornering the market indicates control over a commodity or situation, a term attributable to yesteryear's stock market machinations. Throughout the 19th and well into the 20th century there were no rules against stock market manipulations. Bear raids constituted a favorite pastime, whose object was to panic investors into selling by artificially driving down a stock's price. This was accomplished by selling shares one did not own or "selling short," a practice requiring the borrowing of stock from others. Ideally, one would repurchase these shares at lower prices and return them, along with a lending fee, to their original owners. Naturally the bulls did not sit idly by and often attempted to "corner" the short sellers by pushing prices back up. On certain occasions they succeeded admirably, **cornering the market** and forcing the "shorts" to buy back borrowed shares at horrendous losses. Short selling remains perfectly legal, except that past excesses have been curbed by technical short selling rules imposed by the Securities and Exchange Commission in the 1930s.

In the Limelight
Wet Blanket
Bringing Down the House
Fits the Bill
Stealing One's Thunder
Break a leg
Playing to the Gallery
Peanut Gallery

One of the world's oldest known theaters was dedicated to Dionysus in Athens around 500 B.C. Other cultures built similar structures consisting of stages surrounded by semicircles of rising stone steps. Centuries passed before our more familiar form emerged although proper lighting remained a problem until electricity became widely available. By the early 1800s some progress along these lines became evident when candlelight's mediocre illumination and disastrous fire potential (wet blankets were kept on hand to protect actors) was replaced by more innovative lighting systems. In 1816 Thomas Drummond invented a process which provided brilliant white light by heating lime to incandescence. The end results were quite satisfactory, performers were now able to ply their trade **in the limelight**, and party poopers became our modern day **wet blankets**.

Ancient theaters were primitive but solidly built compared to the ramshackle performance halls of later vintages. Wild applause from enthusiastic audiences, or stamping feet protesting delays, actually possessed the potential of **bringing down the house**. Modern-day construction methods protect us from this negative possibility, while well received offerings often receive accolades indicating that the performance **brought down the house**.

In 1709 unsuccessful playwright John Dennis first produced authentic sounding thunder for the stage. When his technique was pirated for a Macbeth production, Dennis complained that his own works went unheeded while they "**steal my thunder**," a technique currently utilized by performers attempting to upstage each other. Years ago space on advertising hand bills was similarly usurped by those maneuvering to have a description of their talents **fit the bill**, meaning that no room was left for displaying the accomplishments of others.

Just before opening curtain, actors and actresses are often advised to **break a leg**. This rather unusual exhortation is traceable to eighteenth century theatrical productions organized for the benefit of prominent socialites or royalty. Special recognition accorded the performers by the upper crust was repaid with an unusual bow which placed one leg directly behind the other, a maneuver that entertainers dubbed **breaking a leg**.

At one time the cheapest or "gallery" theater seats were populated by rowdy, peanut-munching characters who pelted performers with peanuts whenever lines were spoken too softly. In self defense actors and actresses increased their vocal output, an act of appeasement we now refer to as **playing to the gallery**. Movies and popcorn may have replaced theaters and peanuts as preferred entertainment mediums, but seats furthest from the silver screen continue to be located, as in their theatrical counterparts, in the **peanut gallery**.

Gerrymander
Lame Ducks
Pork Barrel
Lobbyist

The name of Elbridge Gerry does not automatically come to mind whenever we review the political history of our country. Few of us realize that Gerry, who was born in 1744, served America with distinction throughout his entire life.

As a young man, Gerry agitated against British colonial rule and ultimately became a member of the Continental Congress as well as a signer of the Declaration of Independence. His political career continued in the United States Congress, followed by two terms as the governor of Massachusetts. From 1812 until his death in 1814, Elbridge Gerry served James Madison as his vice-president.

Unfortunately, Gerry is best remembered for an episode that occurred during his third quest for the Massachusetts Statehouse. While presiding over the state legislature, Elbridge Gerry changed the boundary lines of certain electoral districts, giving him a decided advantage over his political opponent. A long, skinny district map emerged to which the artist Gilbert Stuart added legs, proclaiming it to be a salamander. Shortly thereafter Benjamin Russell, a newspaper editor favoring the opposing party, immortalized Gerry's name by substituting **Gerrymander** for salamander.

Even if Gerry had lived to complete his term as vice president he would have been unable to preside over a **lame duck** congress or initiate **pork barrel** projects, because neither expression arrived on our political scene until the 1860s. Originally, **lame ducks** had nothing to do with either politicians or ducks. They were members of the London Stock Exchange who had been forced to sell their seats in order to pay off debts.

Prior to 1933 members of Congress or presidents who failed in November re-election bids served until the following March 4th, affording ample time for handing out lucrative contracts to special interests. The image of packing all this "pork" into a barrel for carefully planned dispensation created the **pork barrel** concept. At the same time the unseated and crippled, but not yet powerless, politicians became **lame ducks**.

Most proposed **pork barrel** legislation would quickly fade away for lack of support were it not for the unrelenting pressure applied to members of Congress by highly skilled **lobbyists**. Ever since Civil War days, high ranking government officials and congressmen have tended to congregate in Washington's Willard Hotel for both relaxation and informal business meetings. Early on, citizens seeking to curry favor realized that haunting the lobby of this famous establishment provided ongoing opportunities for waylaying those legislators most likely to be sympathetic to their various causes. Over time this casual practice evolved into a highly sophisticated profession, whose members, perhaps in deference to their humble beginnings in the Hotel Willard's lobby, now call themselves **lobbyists**.

Our constitution originally provided for a four-month turnover time since newly elected office holders required weeks to settle affairs, saddle their horses, and ride to Washington. The advent of modern transportation, coupled with a desire to rid ourselves of **lame duck** antics, gave rise to the Twentieth amendment, moving the March 4th date to January 20th. Even though this change narrowed the window of opportunity for **lame ducks** and their **pork barrel** operations, the practice did more than just survive; it mutated to levels of sophistication undreamed of by our predecessors.

Turnpike
Piker
It Didn't Pan Out
Pay Dirt
Petered Out
Not a Chinaman's Chance
The Acid Test

Around 1800 people of Asian ancestry started migrating to our west coast where they experienced combinations of both incredible hardships and remarkable opportunities. They settled in what was to become California and were later joined by immigrants from other parts of North America, many of whom had used private roads or **turnpikes** to speed their journey. Wagon owners and riders on horseback paid tolls at entrances to rotating barriers of staves or "pikes," while those on foot usually passed free. A number of the latter were not far removed from the vagrant category and were christened **pikers**, a name that has continued to be associated with all varieties of cheapskates and freeloaders.

The 1848 discovery of gold at Sutter's Mill resulted in one of history's great stampedes, forcing Congress to authorize a twenty-dollar gold coin just to absorb the unanticipated flow of precious metal. In order to secure legal title to potential discoveries, prospectors were required to file claims covering their areas of interest. After completing these formalities, a variety of mining techniques were employed, including the panning for gold in rivers. Failure to achieve profitability was often recorded with **it didn't pan out**, the same words we use today for justifying our unrealized expectations.

Blasting powder, a mixture of saltpeter, charcoal and sulfur, provided access to rich strata of gold bearing ore commonly referred to as **pay dirt**. After all commercially viable **pay dirt** was recovered, investors usually concluded their mines were **petered out** and moved on in search of greener pastures. "Chinamen," a generic name for all Orientals, possessed limited economic options and often occupied these abandoned sites hoping for a miracle. Successful rejuvenation of **petered out** mines was such a rarity that **not a Chinaman's chance** became synonymous with all endeavors encumbered by insurmountable odds.

Successful miners had to pass **the acid test** in order to sell their gold dust. Nitric acid, which reacts with all metals except gold, was used to insure that offerings were not diluted with foreign matter. Gold prospectors may be virtually extinct, but **the acid test** survives for measuring both our determination and our fellow man's intentions.

Trivia
Not Worth His Salt
Crossing the Rubicon
The Die is Cast
Burning Your Bridges Behind You
The Point of No return
Pushing the Panic Button

The reign of Publius Aelius Hadrianus, better known to us as Hadrian, spanned the years A.D. 117 to 138 and coincided with the zenith of that civilization's greatness. Under Hadrian's leadership, Rome consolidated her territorial gains, effectively turning the Mediterranean into her private lake. Maintenance of this desirable status quo depended on Rome's extensive system of paved roads along which riders moved information at an astonishing pace. Current news was posted wherever three roads intersected, although what might have been newsworthy to some obviously did not impress others since "tri via" or "three roads" in Latin, has been handed down to us as **trivia**.

Pax Romana was enforced by Rome's many legions. When hard coinage was unavailable, compensation for her soldiers sometimes took the form of plunder from uncooperative frontier regions. On other occasions salt was used as a medium of exchange, which is why we categorize those failing to pull their weight as **not worth their salt**.

Rome's persistent climb to undisputed ruler of the Western world required more than eight hundred years and, until Julius Caesar seized power in 49 B.C., her government operated along the lines of a Republic. Throughout this period, civilian authority was maintained with an unwritten law forbidding generals and their armies to cross the Rubicon, a river in the northern part of the Italian peninsula. Caesar blatantly broke this covenant by announcing "**the die is cast**, I have **crossed the Rubicon**." In order to stiffen his soldiers' resolve, Caesar took the additional provocative step of **burning his bridges behind him**. Rome's citizenry was evidently primed to accept its fate passively since nobody **pushed the panic button** after Julius Caesar's armies reached **the point of no return**.

Crossing the Rubicon, the die is cast, and burning your bridges behind you are self explanatory. The origins of the point of no return and pushing the panic button are of a more recent vintage and may surprise some readers.

During World War II targets in Germany were often so far from England that it was more expedient for bombers to land in territory controlled by the Soviet Union than to return home. This was especially true for commanders of damaged aircraft, who were afforded no choice but to press on once the half way point or, point of no return, had been exceeded. Pilots coping with disabled bombers whose intercom systems had also failed possessed the option of activating a bail out alarm signal by depressing a cockpit panic button. Fifty years later memories of World War II are fading rapidly except that panic button pushers, sensing they have passed their own personal point of no return, appear to remain with us on an indefinite basis.

Hell on Wheels
From the Wrong Side of the Tracks
Jerkwater Town
Fall Asleep at the Switch
Keeping an Ear to the Ground
Featherbedding

On May 10, 1869, tracks laid by the Central Pacific and Union Pacific Railroads were joined with a golden spike at Promontory, Utah, forging the final link in America's first transcontinental railroad. The logistical nightmares inherent in an undertaking of this magnitude had been resolved with the invention of mobile eating, sleeping, and entertainment facilities that moved just behind the work trains. Everything imaginable went on in these unusual conveyances, earning them the sobriquet of **hell on wheels**. America's railroad construction peaked in the early years of the twentieth century, after which the designation of **hell on wheels** was transferred to unmanageable, out-of-control, teenagers.

During America's unbridled era of railroad expansion, the prosperity of numerous hamlets became so dependent on route decisions that they competed heavily for the privilege of having their communities bisected by steel rails. Most towns were already divided into "good" and "bad" areas, and railroad tracks added the ultimate barrier. Ever since, our least fortunate citizens have lived on or come **from the wrong side of the tracks**, along with all those classified by the local establishment as socially unacceptable.

Steam locomotives required periodic infusions of water, a need that did not always coincide with scheduled stops. Water towers placed alongside the tracks at appropriate intervals dispensed this essential commodity with a jerk on a long cord attached to a metal tube. As time went by small communities or **jerkwater towns** sprung up around these facilities, making it difficult for later generations to resist the temptation of calling insignificant or unimportant villages, **jerkwater towns**.

Major portions of each transcontinental route consisted of a single track served by strategically placed sidings for facilitating two-way traffic. Switching trains onto sidings became the responsibility of train crewmen or permanently stationed employees. No more need be said concerning the consequences should any of these minions **fall asleep at the switch**.

The plains Indians were at first frightened, and then saddened, by the advent of the iron horse after realizing that this smoke-belching monstrosity was destined to forever change their way of life. Once the initial shock subsided, some native Americans did become fascinated with this intruder and, unlike the white folk, had no need to consult train schedules. **Keeping an ear to the ground** provided them with all necessary information, and those of us displaying penchants for garnering advance information have likewise learned to credit our success to the practice of **keeping an ear to the ground**.

Steam's demise in favor of diesel power created major labor disputes regarding job security. Acrimonious negotiations ensued, with unions winning a major victory requiring all diesel trains to continue carrying superfluous firemen. Soon afterwards, locomotive engineers made additional demands regarding work area comfort and safety, causing a railroad representative to explode with, "what else do you want up there, a featherbed?"

This semi-amusing incident created **featherbedding** as a new and instantly successful word for describing circumstances whereby employees must, by law, be paid for performing tasks deemed unnecessary by management.

Ku Klux Klan
Carpetbaggers

After the close of the American Civil War, secret societies sprang up in the south for the purpose of opposing Reconstruction measures passed by the United States Congress. One of these organizations, or **Klans**, came to realize that its strange rituals and white-hooded uniforms also served to intimidate their black neighbors. This unanticipated power became the catalyst for a vastly expanded membership, whose primary activity now centered on terrorizing Negroes attempting to exercise their newly won civil liberties and Northern whites seeking to profit from the post-war chaos.

Firearms of that era were discharged by releasing a cocked hammer onto a percussion cap. Ratcheting the hammer backwards to its firing position produced three loud, distinctive, and threatening clicks sounding like **Ku, Klux, Klan**. It is conceivable that this ominous, fear inspiring noise may have motivated the fanatical **Klan** members to preface their name with **Ku** and **Klux**. In the 1870s this infamous organization was actually disbanded, although its unfortunate revival in subsequent years has continued to perpetuate an atmosphere of bigotry and hatred that remains very much in evidence even today.

Upon cessation of hostilities, uninvited opportunists of every persuasion poured into the Southern states. Using legal but immoral and unorthodox methods, these adventurers managed to accumulate vast amounts of property and political influence for virtually nothing. Popular at the time were large baggy valises or carpet bags, so named after their resemblance to floor covering material. With room for a reasonable amount of clothing and light enough to allow for hasty retreats, this luggage was admirably suited to its purpose. Carpetbags soon became associated with, and identified as belonging to, those taking unfair advantage of the law. Unscrupulous individuals were thus anointed with the unusual name of **carpetbagger** that was, and continues to be, reserved for speculators using legal loopholes for excessive personal gain.

Being over a Barrel
Toeing the Party Line

An enormous economic, educational, and social gap existed between officers and crew in the Royal Navy throughout its era of wooden ships and iron men. The former were products of society's most elevated strata, whereas the latter often included the dregs of humanity. Wartime conditions submerged these differences when survival depended on genuine cooperation between all ranks. Peacetime presented a different scenario, with officers and common seamen barely tolerating each other, and the seeds of mutiny lurking continuously just below the surface.

All hands were required to witness the brutal punishment considered necessary for maintaining control over tense and sullen crews. Flogging was prescribed for a variety of offenses and administered to recipients while tied over cannon barrels. In order to mask their own fears, observers of these sadistic spectacles developed tendencies to joke with one another concerning the unpleasant aspects of **being over a barrel**. Passage of time has altered this expression's usage, and **being over a barrel**, or **having someone over a barrel**, now refers to legal problems or financial difficulties rather than physical discomfort.

While attending both punishment sessions and formal ceremonies, sailors were required to stand at attention with bare feet lined up on specific deck seams. They were thus made to **toe the line**, a figure of speech later borrowed by politicians for admonishing party members guilty of exhibiting independent political thoughts. Modern-day mavericks, who nevertheless wish to stay in the good graces of the powers that be, are therefore given no choice but to **toe the party line**.

Brainwashing
Let Slip the Dogs of War

In early 1950, Dean Acheson, President Truman's Secretary of State, made a speech implying that America's sphere of influence in the Pacific extended no further than Japan. North Korea's communist leadership took Atcheson's pronouncement at face value, and in June of 1950, with the tacit approval of the (former) Soviet Union, invaded the Republic of South Korea.

South Korea's defense forces, including a token detachment of American troops, were quickly driven into a small pocket around Puson, Korea's southernmost port. North Korea's undisguised aggression afforded the fledgling United Nations an opportunity to pass its first acid test with flying colors as sixteen nations rushed troops into and held on to this last remaining toehold.

Several months later, General Douglas McArthur defied heavy odds by successfully landing an amphibious force at Inchon, a tiny port city located halfway up Korea's west coast. This bold stroke cut communist supply lines, forcing a North Korean retreat to the Chinese border while our troops entertained visions of being home by Christmas. Overlooked in this euphoric setting was that China had become understandably paranoid over the presence of a large, 95 percent American, UN army right on her doorstep. China's massive and unanticipated entry into the fray now turned the tables, and it became our turn to retreat. By mid-1951 the battle lines had stabilized near the original 38th parallel boundary between the two Koreas, after which talks were initiated in order to resolve this conflict.

All outstanding issues except those involving prisoners of war were settled by 1952. The five thousand UN captives held by the Chinese had undergone what could only be translated into English as "a cleansing of one's mind of impure thoughts." With our penchant for short and comprehensive labels, this process naturally became, and has remained, **brainwashing**. While **Brainwashing** turned very few UN soldiers against their countries, a remarkably high percentage of the one hundred thousand communist captives in UN hands showed no desire to return to their respective homelands. China's insistence on forced repatriations collapsed the peace talks, and fighting resumed until mid-1953 when the communist side finally gave in.

American casualties from this strange war numbered fifty-four thousand dead and over one hundred thousand wounded, almost half of which were suffered after the initial peace talks stalled. Today the Korean War is hardly remembered, but those who participated still wonder at our willingness to sacrifice so many young lives for a truce so fragile that the slightest provocation could once again, as in Shakespeare's *Julius Caesar*, "cry havok and **let slip the dogs of war."**

A Hard Row to Hoe
At the End of One's Rope

In 1607 some one hundred adventure seekers disembarked onto the soil of the New World in an attempt to create England's first permanent settlement at Jamestown, Virginia. Even though this initial colonization attempt failed miserably, other intrepid souls eventually managed to secure a toehold on the fringes of the North American Continent. From these humble beginnings, only one hundred and fifty years were to pass before the population on the Atlantic seaboard burgeoned to the astonishing level of one and one half million people.

The western boundary of Great Britain's new dominions consisted of various rugged mountain ranges collectively called the Appalachians. Relatively few families possessed the fortitude to penetrate this formidable barrier, and England did not encourage westward expansion because protecting new settlements was too expensive. Latecomers thus belatedly discovered that most remaining cheap or free farmland was of substandard quality, a circumstance guaranteeing economic failure unless every family member contributed to the fullest extent. Each child was therefore given a hoe and responsibility for cultivating a row of crops, the back breaking nature of which elicited complaints that he or she had **a hard row to hoe**.

In the early 1800s roads, canals, and later railroads created access to vast tracts of fertile western farmland. Presumably the quality of farm children's lives improved as well. Be that as it may, **a hard row to hoe** remains a choice expression for describing the plight of those burdened with intolerable difficulties, although we might also venture that those in dire straights are **at the end of their rope**.

The image conveyed by **at the end of his rope** of some unfortunate soul dangling from a noose is incorrect. Most farms possessed grazing animals that were routinely pressed into lawnmower service. Tying these creatures to long ropes not only kept them from running away but also produced more or less evenly cropped lawns. Needless to say, the more adventuresome animals could often be observed straining to sample horizons beyond the range of their tethers. The complexity of today's society is such that individuals, beset with frustration over limitations or circumstances beyond their control, often find themselves **at the end of their rope** as well.

Throwing Down the Gauntlet
Picking Up the Gauntlet
A Horse of a Different Color
Passing With Flying Colors

Throughout Europe's middle ages, wealthy communities periodically hosted tournaments enabling knights to display their racing, jousting, sword play, and archery skills. Injuring opponents was not part of the game plan, although accidents were inevitable whenever riders holding lances the size of small telephone poles approached each other at full tilt. Just as in sports today, emotions were not always kept in check, causing challenges to be issued in order to resolve differences of opinion.

Custom required the observation of certain conventions before grudge matches could proceed. Challenges were initiated by **throwing down the gauntlet**, a metal-covered leather glove. Acceptance was signaled by **picking up the gauntlet**, a physical effort of some magnitude when encased in a full suit of armor. Strenuous activities of this nature and their accompanying formalities have now faded into the distant past, which is not to say we haven't retained our propensity for dealing with threatening situations by throwing down or picking up gauntlets in a mental sense.

Horses participating in racing events were decked out in multitudes of bright colors. Favorites did not always live up to expectations and, when unexpected colors flashed across the finish line, disappointed spectators were quick to proclaim "that's **a horse of a different color**." Coping within our present-day environment, we register surprise in a similar manner whenever the outcome of events thought to be lead pipe cinches undergo unexpected transformations.

As children we are taught, and therefore politely pretend, that playing the game is what really counts, even though deep down all of us prefer winners over losers. Racing events may end with every mounts' colors flapping in the breeze, but in the world of humans only individuals exhibiting outstanding abilities receive the accolade of having **passed with flying colors**.

Graybacks
Bluebacks
Greenbacks
Don't Take Any Wooden Nickels
Putting in Our Two Cents' Worth
Close but No Cigar

Every schoolchild learns that Confederate currency, known as **graybacks** or **bluebacks**, became worthless well before the Civil War's end. Not generally realized is that the Union's new **greenbacks** also fared poorly. Excessive distribution of this medium of exchange debased its value, driving gold, silver, and even copper coins out of circulation. The resulting void was filled by pressing postage stamps, fractional notes, and tokens into service as small change. When new coins were proposed in 1865 to redeem this substitute currency, nickel mining interests successfully promoted a bill creating three-cent and five-cent pieces specifying a 75 percent copper, 25 percent nickel composition.

Although the three-cent coin was abandoned in 1889, nickels have thrived to our present day. In 1883 the nickel's original design was changed to a liberty head obverse and a large Roman V reverse, from which the words five cents were deleted. Five-dollar gold pieces sported a similar liberty head obverse, and the coins were virtually identical in size, enticing con artists to gold plate the new nickels before passing them off as the real McCoy. Even though the design error omitting five cents was corrected within the same year, public suspicion regarding nickel coins persisted.

Throughout this same general time frame, wooden nickels were handed out as souvenirs at county fairs. Since they obviously had no value and the gold plated nickel fiasco was still fresh in people's minds, adults began using **don't take any wooden nickels** for warning their children to avoid spurious schemes.

These same fairs provided a variety of games for testing strength and coordination, including one whose objective was to ring a bell by driving a heavy weight up a pole. Success was rewarded with a cigar, while failure produced the monotonous chant of **close but no cigar**. Ever since, whenever anticipated goals are narrowly missed, there always seems to be a wise-guy standing in the wings with his own special version of **close but no cigar.**

Throughout the nineteenth century, the United States Mint issued many unusual coins including three-cent silver pieces, half cents, gold dollars, twenty-cent pieces, and two-cent coins. Since the two-cent piece was short-lived and unsuccessful, and because we realize that unsolicited advice is unlikely to be accepted gracefully, we now cautiously preface our suggestions to others with **putting in our two cents' worth.**

Blazer
Tuxedo
Having Something up One's Sleeve
Laughing up One's Sleeve
All Gussied Up
Best Bib and Tucker

Captains in the Royal Navy not only paid for their crews' cere-monial uniforms but also competed to produce memorable outfits, many of which used their ships names as motifs. The poor crewmembers of H.M.S. *Tulip* could attest to the fact that these efforts were often less than satisfactory after their tulip costumes made them the fleet's laughing stock. One captain managed to dis-play an unusual talent for design by providing his men with beau-tiful dark blue jackets. The envy of all, these lucky sailors became known as **blazers** after their ship H.M.S. *Blazer*.

Wherever one finds **blazers**, **tuxedos** will surely be close at hand. In the 1880s the well-known Lorillard tobacco family decid-ed to create an exclusive enclave near Tuxedo, New York. Their efforts produced the Tuxedo Park Association, which provided wealthy families with private lakes, clubs, and beautiful homes. Parties given by these original Tuxedo Park residents required very formal attire, and on one such occasion the younger genera-tion protested by cutting off the bottom portion of their long coats or "tails." Harper's magazine made the most out of the resulting uproar by popularizing what they dubbed the "tuxedo coat." In time the establishment grudgingly recognized the need for less formality, thus legitimizing the **tuxedo** as a standard part of one's wardrobe.

When it came to dress codes, citizens living in the 1800s were more fortunate than their fifteenth century counterparts. In those earlier days, men's clothing was very loose, devoid of pockets, and thoroughly impractical. Possessions were carried about on one's belt or nestled in the upper garment's voluminous sleeves. In the same century, almost everyone had such terrible teeth that loud guffawing and showing of molars was not considered to be "de rigueur." Excessive laughter was therefore muffled and unsightly teeth were hidden by the simple expedient of turning head towards sleeve. Because fifteenth century garments served to hide not only teeth but also objects, laughter, and emotions, our language has maintained **having something up one's sleeve** and **laughing up one's sleeve** for expressing mistrust of other people's intentions.

Sometimes we enjoy getting **all gussied up** (from a "gusset" or comfort-enhancing extra piece of cloth) in our **best bib and tucker**. Bibs became a part of men's attire in the seventeenth century and, as the name implies, were used to keep food from spilling onto clothing. Tuckers, or lace shawls for keeping the evening chill from invading ladies' necks, became popular in the same century. We should therefore remember to use this particular colloquialism selectively because a couple can sally forth in their **best bib and tucker**, but any one person attempting this feat might be accused of belonging to a most peculiar persuasion.

Carrying Coals to Newcastle
Rearranging Deck Chairs on the *Titanic*
Fiddling While Rome Burns

Frustrations resulting from our inability to resolve knotty problems sometimes cause us to announce that we might as well be **carrying coals to Newcastle** or **rearranging deck chairs on the *Titanic***.

Early in the thirteenth century, entrepreneurs from the town of Newcastle realized that their community's ample coal deposits, located alongside the tidal river Tyne, guaranteed an unparalleled competitive advantage. Their 1239 petition to King Henry III for mining rights was successful, allowing Newcastle to become the world's first coal port. Prosperity followed, especially after the emergence of the industrial revolution and its accompanying rise in manufacturing activity. By the early twentieth century, Tyne's importance had dwindled relative to other English industrial cities, but not before giving us **carrying coals to Newcastle** as a most satisfactory combination of words to express contempt for activities deemed to be totally superfluous.

The astonishing story of an unsinkable ship named *Titanic* that nevertheless died during her maiden voyage in the cold North Atlantic on April 15, 1912, is too well known to require repetition. With the benefit of hindsight, chronicles depicting this remarkable tragedy uniformly agree the *Titanic's* fate was irreversibly sealed moments after a collision with an iceberg ruptured all her forward watertight compartments. **Rearranging deck chairs on the *Titanic*** became the disaster's most famous colloquial legacy, one which is often directed against individuals suspected of spending inordinate amounts of time on projects promising zero chance of success.

Unsupported records suggest that Nero instigated Rome's great fire in A.D. 64 for the dual purpose of satisfying his instant urban renewal cravings and to fabricate additional reasons for persecuting Christians. History censured Rome's emperor for taking no action and **fiddling while Rome burned**, despite the fact that containing a conflagration of such magnitude would have been clearly impossible. The bottom line of this tale is that while Nero's degree of culpability can never be adequately ascertained, we nevertheless persist in accusing those immobilized by calamity of **fiddling while Rome burns**.

Bug Out
On Tenterhooks
Listen Up

While writing this book, the realization struck me that I personally participated in events which took place soon after the creation of **bug out**, a phrase commonly used to describe hastily conceived, spur of the moment retreats.

Forty-five years ago the Korean "police action" mushed to a halt through the implementation of a tenuous, often violated, truce that has yet to be transformed into a meaningful peace agreement. A number of us arrived on the scene shortly thereafter and were assigned to the U.S. Army's Second Division as paymasters. Our duties placed us just behind the newly established demilitarized zone where we prepared monthly payrolls to be picked up by commanders of front line units. Tense moments on the DMZ often prevented officers from leaving their posts, providing us with opportunities to pay the troops in person. Needless to say, the possibility of full-scale resumption of hostilities kept us **on tenterhooks** throughout our entire tour of duty.

At one time newly produced cloth was stretched on wooden frames or "tenters" equipped with "tenterhooks" for holding wet cloth in place. As the years passed, tenters became obsolete, although the concept of being **on tenterhooks** survived for portraying ongoing, suspenseful, mentally stretching situations.

Our immediate superiors in Korea were attuned to reality by recognizing that support unit personnel were seldom endowed with a proper sense of military tradition or fighting spirit. Keeping us up to scratch required "rearward deployment drills," which were sporadically announced with the terse command of **bug out**. The top brass held this phrase in low esteem because it was born of desperation during the war's early days, but we nevertheless learned to **listen up** and prepare for evacuation whenever **bug out** was shouted through the door of our Quonset hut. Since there was never a guaranty that this was not just another drill, and because all of us were much more proficient with adding machines than M-1 rifles, the **bug out** command was always obeyed with unsurpassed enthusiasm.

History does repeat itself with monotonous precision. The

Korean experience should have weaned us from military adventures lacking well-defined objectives, the will to win, and at least a modicum of public support. Korea's hard won lesson was ignored as, only half a generation later, we embroiled ourselves in the even more frustrating Vietnam War. Throughout previous conflicts, new information or instructions had been disseminated to our troops with "gather round" or "pay attention." In Vietnam the byword changed to **listen up**. One may speculate that **listen up** became popular because rapidly changing field conditions required more efficient language. Whatever the reason, probably our least painful reminder of this controversial conflict has been that both military and civilian announcements are now invariably prefaced with **"listen up."**

There'll be the Devil to Pay
Being at Loggerheads
Running the Gauntlet

Boats may be aptly described as holes in the water into which one pours money and, because of continuous maintenance requirements, wooden ships of old fit this description even better than our current fiberglass or steel-hulled models. Caulking or "paying" the seams on sailing vessels required vast expenditures of human effort as well as specialized tools called "loggerheads." These instruments consisted of long iron rods with knobs on one end which were heated, dipped in pitch or tar, and then applied to the appropriate area. The word "pay" is traceable to the French "peier," meaning to cover with hot tar. Whenever this material failed to arrive on time, crewmen commented, "there'll be the devil (the first plank above the waterline) to pay and no hot pitch." Somehow, **there'll be the devil to pay** survived as a shortened version of this factual statement for promising dire consequences to those of us neglecting our duties.

Competition among crew members racing the clock to finish their assigned sectors was often intense, and arguments regarding winners or losers were commonplace because neatness counted as much as speed. At times these disputes turned into ugly brawls resulting in the use of loggerheads as weapons. Luckily, the physical aspects of **being at loggerheads** have been replaced with verbal indications of hopeless deadlock, forcing participants to **run the gauntlet** in an emotional sense in order to resolve their differences.

Running the gauntlet originated as a form of punishment in the Swedish army. Soldiers subjected to this form of discipline were forced to run naked down a narrow path bordered on both side by men swinging large clubs. Combining the Swedish words for a narrow path and running produced "gattlope," later to become "gauntlet." Interestingly enough, there is no connection between this type of gauntlet and the kind we throw down or pick up. The Swedish army now employs more sophisticated methods for chastening mavericks, while **running the gauntlet** is reserved for describing the mental anguish that often accompanies difficult decisions.

Ponzi Scheme
Tulipmania
South Sea Bubble

It seems that every several months financial publications such as *The Wall Street Journal* reveal the existence of new, ever more sophisticated **Ponzi schemes**. Occasionally these same information sources will supplement their **Ponzi scheme** disclosures with examples of **Tulipmania** or **South Sea Bubbles**. All of the above allude to fraudulent investment proposals which, in spite of their transparent nature, somehow manage to ensnare wealthy individuals on a regular basis.

Boston's Charles Ponzi first appeared on our economic horizon in 1920 after promising large returns from a mysterious and secretive investment scheme. To everyone's astonishment, Ponzi's original partners raked in monthly profits approaching 50 percent, a largess supposedly made possible by taking advantage of exchange rate fluctuations associated with International Postal Coupons. Evidently no one questioned the impossibility of this arithmetic, and Ponzi regularly moved his operation to more spacious offices as each predecessor filled to the ceiling with cash. In due course, investors perceived that Ponzi was simply paying off one round of participants with contributions supplied by the next wave of suckers, an expedient ultimately destined for failure. The resulting uproar was so spectacular that for the last three quarters of a century the words **Ponzi scheme** have come to describe questionable promotions of all stripes.

Shortly after Ottoman Sultan Mohammed II captured Constantinople (today's Istanbul) in 1453, he beautified his conquest with formal gardens utilizing local wild flowers that we would have recognized as tulips. By the end of the following century, tulips appeared in the Netherlands, a rather mysterious transformation as Asia's hot summers and cold winters presented an anathema to the damp, more moderate climate of the Lowlands.

Initially, rarity and correspondingly high prices limited tulip ownership to those of superior means. Eventually an increasing demand generated additional supplies, resulting in affordable price levels for common types of bulbs. Prices for rare varieties, however, continued to escalate, enticing an otherwise conservative citizenry to enter the fray through organized tulip bulb exchanges. At the height of the 1637 buying frenzy, investors paid up to ten-thousand guilders for a single bulb, pledging entire farms or elegant Amsterdam canal houses as collateral. Shortly thereafter, publicity generated by workmen eating a rare bulb they had mistaken for an onion, instantly ended history's most astonishing financial mania and left Holland's economy in ruins.

In 1711 Great Britain granted the newly formed South Sea Company a trade monopoly with South America and various Pacific islands. Initial success was so remarkable that King George I was appointed CEO and the company offered to absorb England's national debt of fifty million pounds in return for additional trading privileges. Next, the South Sea Company proposed exchanging this newly acquired debt for a secondary stock issue, a proposal that not only found favor with many holders of government paper but also precipitated a wild scramble for the company's stock. Within six months its price soared from 128 to 1000 pounds per share, the directors unloaded, and four months later the inevitable downward spiral bottomed out at 135.

Despite the stock's rollercoaster ride the enterprise continued to prosper, a circumstance that spawned numerous undercapitalized corporate imitations whose shares became completely worthless. This classic combination of investor greed and corporate dishonesty caused the financial demise of untold thousands, creating the **South Sea Bubble** which, as in the case of Holland's **Tulipmania**, shook England's economic foundation to its very core.

Robbing Peter to Pay Paul
Poor as a Church Mouse
Month of Sundays
Eat One's Words
Red Letter Day
When in Rome
Sacred Cow
Blue Laws

In December of 1540, the abbey church of St. Peter, West-minster, was not only upgraded to a cathedral but also received a commensurate increase in revenue producing estates. Unfortunately for its parishioners, St. Peter's enhanced economic status was destined to be short- lived. Within ten years, its diocese was merged with that of St. Paul's in London, after which St. Peter's surplus wealth was regularly siphoned off for maintaining the more important St.Paul's Cathedral. Protests engendered by this underhanded treatment fell on deaf ears, allowing **robbing Peter to pay Paul** to become the generic byword for unethical financial subterfuges.

Places of worship in the seventeenth century may have provided food for the soul but were otherwise barren of creature comforts. Mice abandoning cozy homes for non-existent pickings in churches found themselves so deprived of sustenance that those trapped on the bottom rung of society's economic ladder are now identified as being **poor as a church mouse.**

A month of Sundays means a very long time, to which New England's Puritans could have cheerfully attested. Every Sunday these stoic souls endured not only four-hour morning services but, after a brief respite for mid-day dinner, were subjected to an additional three-hour afternoon session. Their ordeal continued unabated with compulsory evening prayers, while napping was thwarted by minions wielding wooden poles festooned with feathers for tickling and knobs for bashing.

At first blush no one would suppose that the rather crude expression to **eat one's words** might be traceable to our religious heritage. It seems, however, that in 1370 a sinner named Bernabo Visconti was excommunicated by Pope Urban V, who dispatched two emissaries bearing a parchment to that effect. Visconti did not accept his punishment gracefully and forced the unfortunate bearers of bad tidings to eat the entire proclamation, leaden Papal seal included.

Fifteenth century church calendars used red ink for designating certain holidays, saints' days, and other festive occasions. For hundreds of years thereafter, virtually all social activity centered around the church, causing us to classify specific days that altered our lives for the better as **red letter days**.

Our younger generation probably prefers "go with the flow" over **when in Rome** (do as the Romans do). This sage advice was offered to Saint Augustine by Saint Ambrose after the former admitted confusion because Romans fasted on Saturday, a practice that differed from the custom observed in Saint Augustine's home town of Milan.

Cows are considered sacred by Hindus and roam India's streets free from molestation even when hunger stalks the land. Although most Westerners find this devotion difficult to fathom, our language has nevertheless recognized the Hindu faith's incredible discipline by reserving the term **sacred cow** for people, concepts, and projects not to be disturbed or disrupted under any circumstances.

Blue laws are designed to keep us from indulging in activities deemed to be inappropriate for the Sabbath. Use of the word "blue" in this context traces its roots to the American Revolution, during which The Reverend Samuel Peters remained vocally loyal to King George III. His error in judgment resulted in banishment to England, whereupon the reverend retaliated by spreading rumors about the existence of a fictitious blue-bound book replete with petty laws designed to irritate our day of rest.

Achilles' Heel
Cassandra
Cutting the Gordian Knot
Eureka
Halcyon Days
Oedipus Complex-Electra Complex
Opening Pandora's Box
Rich as Croesus
The Midas Touch
Under the Sword of Damocles
Hanging by a Thread

Holding him by one heel, the goddess Thetis dipped Achilles in the river Styx, coating him with an invulnerable shield. During the Trojan War, Paris discovered Achilles' tiny unprotected area and killed him with an arrow shot to the heel. While this is an unlikely story, its perpetuation nevertheless permits us to consider any area of vulnerability an **Achilles' heel**.

The daughter of Priam and Hecuba, Cassandra spurned Apollo who, in a fit of pique, endowed her with an ability to both foresee the future and the certainty that her prophecies would be universally ignored. Cassandra thus failed to convince her peers that Troy was doomed, from whence came the concept of categorizing modern purveyors of doom and gloom as **Cassandras**.

Practical problem solvers tend to employ bold strategies for **cutting the Gordian knot** while their compatriots flounder about in seas of despair. Legend would have us believe that Gordius, the father of King Midas, became king of Phrygia by fulfilling a prophecy that the first man driving a wagon to the temple of Jupiter would rule the land. Overwhelmed by good fortune Gordius dedicated his wagon to Jupiter by attaching it to a temple beam with an intricate knot nobody could unravel. At this crucial moment Alexander the Great just happened to be riding by and **cut the Gordian knot** with one swift, decisive stroke of his trusty sword.

Truth is often stranger than fiction and perhaps this well-documented, probably true tale should be removed from the mythological category. In any case, when King Hiero II of Syracuse took delivery of a new crown, its weight made him suspect that small amounts of silver had been substituted for gold. Archimedes was retained to ferret out the truth, a seemingly impossible task without damaging the crown. As Archimedes entered his bath to ponder this enigma, he noticed his sinking body creating a vast displacement of water, most of which slopped over the tub's edge. Shouting "**Eureka**," the Greek equivalent of "I have found it," he dashed naked through the streets, seemingly oblivious to his surroundings. Archimedes' flash of insight convinced him there was a relationship between displacement and weight, a discovery which led him to correctly conclude that King Hiero's crown was not the real McCoy.

Unbroken stretches of calm, serene, and joyous days might be recorded in one's diary as **Halcyon days**, which, until the end of the fifteenth century, were actually designated as specific dates on the calendar. Alcyone was the Greek god of wind who drowned herself after her husband, Ceyx, perished in a storm. Her suicide angered the other gods who turned Alcyone and Ceyx into halcyons, or birds recognizable today as kingfishers. Taking pity on the luckless couple, Alcyone's father decreed a yearly quota of fourteen tranquil **halcyon days** for breeding purposes, thus guaranteeing survival of the species.

Oedipus' parents, Laius and Jocasta, ruled Thebes but abandoned him as an infant after a soothsayer predicted he would kill his father and wed his mother. Upon entering manhood, Oedipus unknowingly killed his father in a duel and later married his widowed mother, thus unwittingly fulfilling a long-forgotten prophecy. Mythology portrays Oedipus as a tragic figure rather than a pervert, but psychiatrists nevertheless settled on **Oedipus complex** for describing abnormal relationships between mothers and sons, and **Electra complex** for unnatural attractions between daughters and fathers. Electra's saga reads like a soap opera as well. The daughter of Clytemnestra and Agamemnon, she enlisted her brother Orestes to help kill her mother and lover because the latter murdered Agamemnon upon his return from the Trojan Wars.

Exposing a potential crisis to the light of day runs the risk of making matters worse by **opening Pandora's box**. At one time the world contained only motherless male Titans who spawned in the nether regions and clawed their way to the surface through fissures in the rocks. One of these Titans named Prometheus infuriated the gods by stealing fire from the heavens for use on earth. Zeus retaliated by instructing Vulcan to create Pandora, the first woman, while each of the other gods sealed one of mankind's evils in a box for presentation to Pandora's future husband. Prometheus was ordered to marry Pandora but persuaded Epimetheus to take his place. Ignoring Pandora's warning, Epimetheus foolishly opened the box, allowing our collective ills to escape and forever plague the human race.

Whenever we paste the "**rich as Croesus**" label on anyone we are referring to King Croesus, who ruled the city-state of Lydia, located in today's western Turkey, from 560 to 546 B.C. His staggering wealth was accumulated through a combination of conquest, trade, and the invention of coinage. In earlier days business transactions had been consummated with odd-sized lumps of gold or silver requiring constant weighing and inspection. Croesus's coins were recognized and trusted throughout the ancient world because their markings guaranteed both standard weight and specific precious metal content. This revolutionary idea precipitated a vast expansion of trade from which Croesus profited handsomely. Legend records that, despite his accomplishments, Croesus was an unhappy man, whereupon Herodotus counseled that wealth alone did not suffice and one must live a satisfying life in order to find true happiness. This questionable portion of our tale continues with the chronologically insupportable claim that Croesus was later captured by Cyrus but spared from execution by crying out for Herodotus, their mutual friend.

During King Midas's tenure as ruler of Phrygia, he cemented a friendship with Silenus, the god of fertility and wine, by introducing the later to Dionysus. Silenus asked Midas to name his own reward, and, failing to anticipate the consequences, Midas asked that all he touched be turned to gold. The wish was granted, although King Midas soon found himself in great distress since all sustenance solidified into gold upon touching his lips. Hunger vanquished greed, and the king's appeal for relief was answered by Dionysus, who advised him to cleanse himself in the Pactolus river. Midas followed instructions, his curse was lifted, the Pactolus river became a depository of gold-bearing ores, and habitually successful investors became endowed with **the Midas touch**.

The following story tells us why **under the sword of Damocles** or **hanging by a thread** is so frequently used to describe the emotional state of individuals subjected to real or imagined perils. Around 400 B.C. Damocles attended the court of Dionyius, ruler of Syracuse, where he persisted in harping on the degree of happiness Dionyius must be experiencing in the wielding of his considerable power. Dionyius felt a lesson in humility was in order and invited Damocles to a sumptuous state diner. All went well until Damocles glanced up and found himself sitting under a giant sword hanging by a single thread. Paralyzed by fear lest his slightest movement bring down the sword, Damocles suddenly realized that nobody ever escapes the worries and fears which also keep the high and mighty from fully enjoying their superior status.

Barking up the Wrong Tree
Beating Around the Bush
The Lion's Share
Stool Pigeon
Having the Goods on Someone
Cough up On
Fall Guy

Man's best friend is not necessarily smarter than many commonly hunted animals. Just as hounds are closing in for the kill, raccoons have been known to climb a tree, leave their scent, and escape after jumping into the branches of an adjoining tree. The dogs end up **barking up the wrong tree**, something all of us have done time and again.

Bird hunting entails expenditures of vast amounts of energy by man and beast alike because large tree and brush- filled areas must be scoured to flush out potential prey. Naturally **the lion's share** of this work tends to be unproductive, leading us to rebuke those wasting time or not getting to the point for **beating around the bush.**

The lion's share may be attributed to one of Aesop's Fables. It seems a lion and three other animals returned from a hunt, and a division of the spoils was at hand. Mr. Lion announced that as king of the beasts he was entitled to an extra share and that a further one quarter should be reserved for his mate and cubs. The other participants were welcome to divide the remainder—that is, if they could take it away from him.

Several hundred years ago North America was home to billions of passenger pigeons. Hunters periodically blinded captive pigeons, tied long strings to their legs, and then sat on small stools to which the strings' other ends were attached. These live decoys, or **stool pigeons**, attracted flocks of wild pigeons, allowing whole-sale slaughters to take place. Around 1900 the last wild specimen was shot, and its stuffed body remains on view at the Smithsonian Institute.

Nineteenth century police departments used known criminals as decoys or **stool pigeons** for the purpose of luring other suspects within easy reach of the law. Over the years **stool pigeons** changed

145

their role from decoy to informer, positioning themselves to **cough up on** criminals **having the goods on them**. Translated into our vernacular, they apprised the authorities as to the identity and location of criminals possessing stolen goods. Modern usage has changed **cough up** to hand over, while **having the goods on someone** implies possession of specific and damaging knowledge regarding the affairs of others.

Sometimes apprehended suspects become **fall guys** through the simple expedient of serving prison sentences in order to protect their bosses or cohorts. Originally, **fall guys** were not criminals but professional wrestlers paid to made their opponents look good with convincingly contrived defeats.

Black Sheep
Bellwether
Dyed in the Wool
Two Shakes of a Lamb's Tail
Tarred with the Same Brush
Pulling the Wool Over One's Eyes
Might as Well Be Hung for a Sheep

Black sheep tend to be ostracized because black wool is virtually unmarketable and their appearance frightens other animals. Unconventional human beings are often subjugated to a similar fate, forcing them to live out their allotted life span as **black sheep**.

Sheepherders traditionally employ castrated, bell-wearing, or **bellwether** sheep for herding purposes, a term the rest of us favor for describing trendsetters or individuals poised on the cutting edge of new technologies.

After raw wool has been dyed, color changes are difficult to manage. This is why **dyed in the wool** bachelors rarely marry or why **dyed in the wool** advocates of various political philosophies remain fanatically dedicated to their causes.

Most likely no one has ever measured the r.p.m.'s of a lamb's tail, but **two shakes of a lamb's tail** seems to have nevertheless become the norm for recording happenings around us.

Identifying sheep as belonging to any particular flock is accomplished by applying tar to a similar area on each animal's anatomy. Since this activity requires only one brush, we speculate that those sharing the punishment of others, regardless of the degree of guilt, have been **tarred with the same brush**.

While discharging their official duties nineteenth century English judges traditionally wore uncomfortable "wool" wigs. Circumstances producing courtroom agitation sometimes caused this ill-fitting headgear to slip forward and cover a judge's eyes. Victorious lawyers understandably seized the moment, proclaiming their shenanigans to have been instrumental in **pulling the wool over his eyes**.

In England's not so distant past, absconding with either a sheep or a lamb was categorized as a hanging offense. Upon being apprehended for stealing lambs rather than the more valuable sheep, thieves thus came to realize that they **might as well be hung for a sheep**, a lesson we've learned as well whenever society fails to create distinctions between various degrees of criminality.

Carrying a Torch
Rest on Our Laurels

The winners of athletic contests that eventually became known as the Olympics were first recorded in 776 B.C. Named after their place of origin, the ancient Greek city of Olympia, these games took place every four years for the next 1170 years. Interruptions were not tolerated, requiring that even major conflicts be held in abeyance until after the festivities' conclusion. In contrast, one might note that the best we have managed during our twentieth-century wars has been suspension of the games. Around A.D. 394 the Roman Emperor Theodosius prohibited their celebration, ending the longest continuous sports event the world has ever known.

In 1896 a Frenchman named Baron Pierre de Coubertin, helped by the discovery and restoration of the original stadium, realized his life long dream of reviving the games. Thirteen countries entered this first modern Olympiad with the American contingent arriving barely in time. Sailing leisurely towards Greece, they had failed to realized until the very last moment that the Eastern World's Julian calendar was eleven days ahead of theirs.

Frantic efforts to reach Olympia in time drove the American team to the point of exhaustion. Despite this handicap, our athletes garnered nine out of eleven gold medals, leading to yet another embarrassment. In 1896 the United States did not have an official national anthem, a problem the local band solved by playing "Yankee Doodle" time and again.

Overall the games were a great success. Interest grew so rapidly that physical limitations, along with overtures from other countries desiring to provide ever more luxurious facilities, soon moved the Olympics away from Greece. A new tradition did, however, emerge for honoring Greece as the Olympics' founding nation. Each successive Olympiad has been opened with the arrival of a lighted torch carried from Olympia by relays of runners. This passing of the flame from athlete to athlete regardless of terrain or weather constitutes a true labor of love and produced a new colloquialism. **Carrying a torch** for someone now indicates unshakable loyalty or love that continues to burn brightly even if not reciprocated.

Athletic contest winners in the ancient world were rewarded

with sprigs of laurel or laurel wreaths. This modest custom not only kept excessive commercialism at bay but also gives us, once secure in the knowledge of a job well done, the opportunity to **rest on our laurels**.

Sandwich
Crapper
Diesel
Macadam
Peeping Tom
John Hancock

John Montagu, the fourth Earl of Sandwich, appears to have been an unsavory character in more ways than one. His tenure as First Lord of the Admiralty became famous for its incompetence and corruption, while compulsive gambling seems to have been one of his lesser private vices. On one such occasion, Montagu refused to pause for meals and ordered servants to deliver bread and sliced meat directly to the gaming tables. Evidently the Earl never missed a beat of the action as he slapped bread and meat together, wolfing it down to consume the world's first **sandwich**.

Various ancient civilizations developed sophisticated methods for flushing away human wastes, an accomplishment that was neglected and soon forgotten by their successors. The tiresome necessity of trekking to the outhouse thus continued for another millennium before Mr. Crapper patented his flush toilet. American soldiers returning from World War I were sufficiently awed by this English invention that **crapper**, along with its various derivative words, quickly became part of everyone's vocabulary. Incidentally, the surprising aspect of this vignette is that Mr. Crapper's first name was Thomas, not John.

By the end of America's Civil War, New England's dwindling whale population precipitated a desperate search for alternative sources of illuminating oil. Deliverance appeared in the form of a black, smelly, almost tar-like substance that seeped from springs, could be dug out of pits, and was even found by drilling wells. A hastily researched refining process reduced this goo to high-grade lamp oil, saving both our eyesight and the remaining whales. The new technology not only raised economic spirits but also embodied every environmentalist's worst nightmare. Because the internal combustion engine had not yet been invented, gasoline and other worthless by-products from refineries were routinely dumped into rivers and set ablaze. Reliable gasoline engines for light machinery appeared around 1880, while the **diesel** engine developed by Dr. Rudolph Diesel in the 1890s turned out to be perfect for heavy-duty applications. Suddenly gasoline and **diesel** fuel no longer trashed the environment. Instead, these former outcasts became premier fuels for powering the next century's dazzling array of new machinery. Dr. Diesel died relatively young under mysterious circumstances, but not before becoming rich, famous, and bequeathing us his name for use in a generic sense.

John Loudon Macadam (1756-1836) was a man ahead of his time because of his ability to envision and build superior roads by properly addressing the question of drainage. His concept involved placing layers of small irregular stones over a sloping roadbed. Passing traffic finished the job by systematically compacting each layer, squeezing water from the roadbed into drainage ditches. Modern builders speed up this process with steamrollers and subsequently coat the surface with a bituminous material popularly referred to as **macadam**.

Once upon on a time Leofric, Lord of Coventry, imposed taxes so burdensome that even his wife, Lady Godiva, took up the peoples' cause. Leofric jokingly acquiesced to her pleas for relief on the condition that she ride naked through the town, an offer Lady Godiva accepted with alacrity. Preparations for her journey on a white horse were preceded by requests that Coventry's inhabitants close their shutters and stay indoors. In deference to Lady Godiva's sacrifice, every citizen complied except for Tom the tailor, who peeped. The **peeping Tom** was reportedly struck blind for his transgression, while Lord Leofric honored his agreement with a tax reduction.

Document signing is often accompanied by requests that you "place your **John Hancock** right here" and refers to the prominence of John Hancock's signature on our Declaration of Independence. Speculation exists that the leaders of a new nation might, in retrospect, have found fault with Hancock's mercantile activities during the years of pre-Revolutionary confrontation with Great Britain. Quite possibly, John Hancock's bold registry constituted a calculated act promising unwavering support for a noble cause and, at the same time, recording a subtle plea for absolution from past sins.

Pitched Battle
Donnybrook
No Man's Land
Beyond the Pale

References to **pitched battles** may conjure up images of ferocious, non-stop conflicts, but in all actuality they constituted a relatively benign form of military activity. Throughout mankind's steady succession of wars there have been instances when the resulting brutality was tempered by the observance of certain rules of etiquette. Battlefield locations might be agreed to in advance, and fighting was often suspended when it became too dark, hot, cold, or wet. Occasionally combatants pitched their tents on either side of a prearranged **no man's land**, allowing the next day's conflict to be recorded as a **pitched battle**.

Donnybrooks are only slightly less violent than **pitched battles** and take their name from the village of Donnybrook when it was the site of a two-week yearly fair originated by King John in 1204. As the years went by, this annual event degenerated into an increasingly violent, continuous brawl. By 1885 the carnage had become so spectacular that even the hard-drinking, fun-loving Irish were satiated and the fair was abandoned.

In modern wars **no man's land** is analogous to the dangerous, hotly contested, and sometimes inaccessible land mass located between opposing armies. Elsewhere in this book it has been noted that medieval towns invented the concept of knighthood because standing armies were too expensive. These same communities developed an equally cheap and practical method for dealing with criminal elements. Some convicts were executed outside the city walls. Others were permanently ostracized, under pain of death if they returned, by forcing them to walk across the open space or **no man's land** surrounding every city. Population pressures and increasingly powerful artillery eventually made town fortifications obsolete, and only a few examples of this unique architectural style survived the depredations of the ages. One of these may be viewed at Naarden, a small village located east of Amsterdam, Holland. As cities expanded beyond their original walls, superstitious citizens often shunned areas where executions had formerly taken place, a practice that created additional **no man's land**.

By the time Western civilization re-emerged from what we conveniently call "the dark ages," many communities depended on walls of wooden stakes or "pales" (from the Latin *palus*) for defensive purposes. History books would have us believe that sovereigns ruled with absolute authority, when in fact they were often unable to exercise effective control over their subjects beyond their city walls or "pales." The English language ultimately benefited from this shortcoming, allowing us to categorize uncontrollable or unacceptable behavior as **beyond the pale**.

Shake a Leg
Son of a Gun
Stonewalled

Sailors used to lead such lonely lives that overnight female companionship was permitted whenever ships were in port. This privilege did not excuse normal duties, and at first light those in charge of various work details ran between tiers of bunks shouting "show a leg." Dainty female appendages rising from beneath the covers were ignored, whereas owners of large hairy legs were summarily routed out. Eventually "show a leg" was replaced with the more satisfying "**shake a leg**," a cry that has continued to serve its purpose of urging laggards onward.

Although undisturbed during these early hours, the ladies were required to disembark before sailing time. Apparently this regulation was cheerfully ignored since many a vessel managed to sail with a number of the fair sex stashed safely below deck. Long voyages produced predictable results, and babies were often born in curtained-off spaces between two cannon. The captain's attempt to fix responsibility was invariably **stonewalled** by crew members pronouncing that the child, having been born next to a cannon, was a **son of a gun**. While there was hardly an element of surprise attached to these proceedings, the words **son of a gun** nevertheless remain our first choice for expressing astonishment.

The concept of obstructing justice by **stonewalling** is derived from the nickname of Confederate general Thomas Jonathan Jackson. Our Civil War's first battle of Bull Run took place near Washington, and Union forces were so certain of victory that entire families rode out in carriages to observe the proceedings. Federal troops did indeed carry the day until they encountered unbelievably stubborn resistance organized by General Jackson. Union momentum ground to a halt and then turned into a rout, precipitating an embarrassing scramble to safety by soldiers and civilians alike. The defeat was so stunning that President Lincoln feared for Washington itself, while General Jackson earned the well chosen sobriquet of **Stonewall**. In 1863 **Stonewall** Jackson received an additional, but most unfortunate distinction. He became the only general in the Civil War and possibly our entire military history to be accidentally fired on and killed by his own men.

Mind Your Ps and Qs
Beating a Dead Horse

Living and working conditions on our early merchant vessels were extremely harsh, presenting ship owners with great difficulties in terms of acquiring and retaining reliable crews. Incentives were necessary, and it became customary to pay a first month's wage in advance. The lion's share of this windfall inevitably ended up in local pubs, whose owners readily extended credit to heavy drinkers. Whenever a ship's scheduled sailing time drew near, its first mate was presented with a summary of unpaid P's and Q's, shorthand for pints and quarts, to be deducted from wages owed at the conclusion of each voyage.

Most semi-literate seamen could barely distinguish Ps from Qs, tempting dishonest first mates and saloon keepers to change Ps into Qs. Originally used as an admonition to be vigilant regarding money matters, **mind your Ps and Qs** later became a warning that one's social graces were on unacceptably thin ice.

The first month of every voyage was dubbed "dead-horse month" because most sailors, whether they had saved their advance pay or not, imagined they were working for nothing. Celebrating the ending of this depressing period was accomplished by parading a horse's effigy around the deck. Much merriment and ceremony ensued, after which their symbol of release was beaten, hoisted on high, and thrown overboard. The ship's officers generally waited out dead-horse month before assigning special work details, secure in the knowledge that expectations of extra effort during this time frame would be like **beating a dead horse**. Although dead-horse month has disappeared from our maritime scene, the sensation that one is **beating a dead horse** remains for those attempting to influence or change deeply entrenched social, political, or economic trends.

Slush Fund
Scuttlebutt
In the Dog House
A Clean Bill of Health
Taking One Down a Peg
Chewing the Fat
Chewing the Rag

Throughout almost 98 percent of mankind's recorded history sailing ships provided both the fastest and most reliable mode of transportation. This undisputed fact is undoubtedly responsible for the immense legacy of nautical terminology found in many modern languages. While other portions of this book have already touched on numerous sail-related colloquialisms, it seems that one final category covering such fascinating subject matter is both proper an fitting.

During long ocean voyages, excess fat and grease or "slush" was carefully collected and saved for sale upon reaching port. Proceeds accruing from this minor enterprise were deposited in the crew's **slush fund** and used to purchase luxuries. In 1866 Congress expropriated the term **slush fund** for the purpose of describing secret, off-budget items, transforming a heretofore innocent practice into one with sinister implications.

Wooden vessels sported square holes or "scuttles" in their deck edges for efficient sea water drainage. Drinking water barrels or "butts" were likewise incised with scuttles, minimizing and thus conserving the amount of precious water available to thirsty crews at any given time. Gossiping while gathered around the **scuttlebutt** was one of the few pleasures accorded common seamen, after which their modest store of shared information continued on its rounds as **scuttlebutt**.

In the dog house did not originate with irate wives banishing errant husbands to Fido's quarters. Instead, we have the slave trade to thank for this useful addition to our vocabulary. Slaves in transit were monitored from small deck cubicles or "dog houses." Those selected for this onerous duty were often treated with contempt and ostracized by other members of the ship's complement for being **in the dog house**.

The height of individual colors on eighteenth century warships determined the relative importance of each vessel and its commander. A series of pegs served to raise or lower these flags, and captains falling from grace could expect orders requiring their banners to be **taken down a peg**, a practice that has definitely survived the age of wooden men of war.

Before leaving port, ships were routinely inspected and, in the absence of communicable diseases, presented with an official document indicating **a clean bill of health**. Unimpeded entry to the next port of call was thus assured, an important consideration for all concerned. Today, those of us finding ourselves under peer scrutiny likewise breath sighs of relief upon receiving **a clean bill of health**.

Food aboard ship was frequently rationed, causing interminable discussion and grousing among seamen as they vigorously chewed their small morsels of salty, fatty pork. We may therefore thank these hardy souls for inventing the practice of **chewing the fat** and, when tobacco was in such short supply that rags were substituted, **chewing the rag**.

Wall Street
Main Street
Detroit
Hollywood
Madison Avenue
Skid Row
Broadway

Names of certain cities and streets may speak volumes to most Americans, but newcomers unfamiliar with our idioms are often puzzled when confronted with headlines such as "**Main Street** to Suffer from **Wall Street** Bailout." Only later do they realize that **Main Street** represents not a specific location but the collective aspirations of our hard working citizenry, many of whom live in small communities whose most prominent roadway is almost invariably called Main Street.

Wall Street has managed to perpetuate its hold on almost everyone's mind as a synonym for America's wealth, even though the New York Stock Exchange has never enjoyed a permanent Wall Street address. As a matter of fact, only a handful of brokerage houses currently maintain offices on this short but famous thoroughfare, which boasts the unique distinction of starting near a graveyard and ending in a river.

Unwritten laws seemingly dictate that **Detroit** and **Hollywood** must accompany any and all references to the automotive or motion picture industries. Apparently no one cares that Detroit contributes very modestly towards our nation's automotive output, or that only a tiny proportion of America's cinematic offerings presently emanate from Hollywood.

Criticism of the advertising world is often directed against **Madison Avenue**. In 1944 the *New Republic* magazine published an article assessing the role of advertising in the war effort. The write-up was signed **Madison Avenue** because so many major agencies were located on this famous New York City street. The words **Madison Avenue** therefore became, and somehow remain, equated with advertising, often in a negative sense, despite the fact that Madison Avenue advertising addresses are no longer considered stylish.

Upon the conclusion of our Civil War, lumbering operations commenced on a vast scale throughout various regions of the country. Transportation problems were solved by paving primitive roads with greased logs, enabling teams of horses to skid freshly cut timber to saw mills. Around 1920 one such abandoned **skid road** near Seattle became a mecca for numerous run-down saloons and bars, providing a haven for local derelicts and vagrants. **Skid road** contracted to **skidrow** and **skidrows**, populated by society's outcasts, can now be found in communities all across our nation.

New York City's inexorable northward expansion during the eighteenth and nineteenth centuries was accompanied by a string of theaters along Broadway, a wide thoroughfare slicing diagonally through New York's symmetrical grid of streets and avenues. This geographical fact of life served to identify the acting profession with **Broadway**, a relationship which continues to thrive even though few theaters currently display Broadway addresses. Obsolescence destroyed the older facilities while many contemporary structures were converted into movie houses. Most surviving playhouses are currently located in side streets near Times Square, a happenstance that has yet to deter devotees of the limelight from striving to capture leading roles in **Broadway** productions.

Apple Pie Order
Scarce as Hen's teeth
Cool as a Cucumber
Selling Like Hot Cakes
Jaywalker
Setting One's Cap
Eating Crow
Doing a Land Office Business
I'll Be There with Bells On
Sleep Tight

The Pilgrims' survival of their first New England winter confirmed that one could indeed carve a new life from the harsh lands lying across untold miles of inhospitable ocean. Two hundred and fifty years later, thousands of settlements stretched across the width and breadth of the North American Continent. This miracle was made possible by self sufficiency in all fields of endeavor, including culinary skills. The latter were routinely displayed through community baking contests, whose participants became so expert that just good-tasting apple pies no longer qualified for kudos. Instead, top honors accrued to those presenting the most immaculately executed designs, and we thus have our talented ancestors to thank for the opportunity of equating neatness and exactness with **apple pie order**.

Combining common sense and necessity helped many a pioneer family through rough patches and also created an earthy sense of humor. Anything in short supply became **scarce as hen's teeth** because hens don't have teeth. **Cool as a cucumber** turned out to be more accurate since a cucumber's insides are actually some twenty degrees cooler than the surrounding air. We are likewise indebted to our forefathers for **selling like hot cakes**, a well-worn cliché relating to the rate at which hungry farmers demolished stacks of pancakes in the wee hours of each working day.

As villages grew larger, thousands of bluejays, which had previously mingled freely with horses and humans, fled to the boondocks where they somehow became identified with unsophisticated country folk. On their infrequent visits to town the latter were often overwhelmed by their surroundings and wandered about in a daze, unmindful of dangers presented by roaring wagons and dashing horses. Local denizens found this spectacle most entertaining and christened those caught in the crossfire as **jaywalkers**.

Unmarried ladies often wore small caps not unlike those foisted upon parlor maids in years to come. Part of the preening process in anticipation of a favorite swain's visit included proper positioning of this headgear, a custom that survived figuratively as **setting one's cap** towards the goal of achieving specific objectives.

Settlers were periodically called to arms and the concept of being humbled, or **eating crow**, has been attributed to one such occasion. During a truce in our 1812 war with Great Britain, an American soldier shot a crow within enemy lines. An English officer sallied forth pretending to admire the kill and asked to inspect the Yankee's musket. The latter foolishly complied, found his weapon leveled against him and was forced to eat part of the crow to atone for violating British territory. After retrieving his rifle, the American then turned the tables on his tormentor by requiring him to **eat crow** as well.

As each new Western territory opened to frantic hordes of free land seekers, government-run land offices were established for parceling out land and recording claims. Demands for their services were so enormous that other successful enterprises took to announcing their own prowess with boasts of **doing a land office business**.

Despite the many supplicants, there was usually enough land for all, leaving ranch and farm houses well separated from one another. Communication was problematic, although the word somehow got around whenever a good party was in the offing. In spite of these difficulties, hosts could nevertheless accurately anticipate their guests' arrival time, because carriage horses were draped with bells whose sound carried for miles over the clean, clear air. Years later the telephone replaced word of mouth invitations, after which acceptances came to be prefaced with **I'll be there with bells on**.

Dangerous after-dark return trips were avoidable with overnight stays and, upon preparing to retire, guests were often advised to **sleep tight**. This exhortation was not a suggestion to get drunk but rather a guarantee that a good night's rest awaited because the host had assiduously tightened their mattress-supporting bed frame ropes.

Third World Countries
It's a Whole New Ball Game
Bottom Line
Surfing the Net
Technological Innovations

The process never stops. Some popular expressions have graced our presence for half a millennium. Other examples, such as **third world countries, it's a whole new ball game**, and **bottom line**, are actually much younger than one might suppose.

The closing days of World War II ushered in the "cold war," a bitter and sometimes violent conflict between the Western democracies and Communist block countries competing for the hearts and minds of populations residing in various non-aligned nations. Some of the latter quickly chose sides, while others cleverly garnered even more foreign aid by spurning all advances. In time the financial machinations of these high stake players earned them the collective title of **third world countries**. In due course the superpowers tired of playing economic chicken, shifting the label of **third world countries** to the least successful, most backward of our planet's societies.

It's a whole new ball game and **bottom line** are no older than young adults, while **surfing the net** has yet to progress beyond diapers. **It's a whole new ball game** has been attributed to Henry Kissinger's 1960s Middle East peace mediations, and **bottom line** emerged from President Nixon's 1970s Watergate hearings. Relatively few people know or care where the Internet came from, who owns it or how it functions, but millions throughout the world have unquestionably become addicted to **surfing the net**.

Every technological advance raises expectations which then require language revisions in order to distinguish between new products and their closely related predecessors. **Wireless transmission** appeared on the scene shortly after radio supplanted many telegraphic functions. Motion picture sound tracks combined with Technicolor to give us **silent films** and **black and white movies**. Faded from use but worthy of mention are the **iron horse** and the **horseless carriage**. The introduction of color T.V. sets produced references to a previous dark age of **black and white** television. **Cordless telephones** abound; **e-mail** and **voice-mail** threaten the standard kind: and, who knows, perhaps future generations will ponder how previous civilizations survived the primitive days of **phoneless automobiles, unairconditioned homes,** or **faxless public facilities.**

Epilogue

Upon commencing this project I naively assumed I would be hard pressed to unearth more than a modest quota of worthy colloquialisms, quotations, and words. To my astonishment it soon became apparent that they numbered in the thousands rather than hundreds, and that new examples will be destined to ingrain themselves into our speech patterns even before this book comes to rest on anyone's coffee table. I must therefore reluctantly conclude that no one work can conceivably do justice to the volume of material at hand, and offer most humble apologies to any reader whose favorite phrases have somehow been excluded.

References

Ciardi, John. *A Browser's Dictionary.*
New York: Harper & Row Publishers, Inc.,1980.

Craig, Hardin, ed. *The Complete Works of Shakespeare.*
Chicago: Scott Foresman & Co., 1951.

Espy, Willard R. *Thou Improper, Thou Uncommon Noun.*
New York: Clarkson & Potter Inc., 1978.

Feldman, David. *Who Put the Butter in Butterfly.*
New York: Harper & Row Publishers, Inc., 1989.

Funk, Charles Earl. *Thereby Hangs a Tale.*
New York: Harper & Row Publishers, Inc., 1958.

Funk, Wilfred. *Word Origins and Their Romantic Stories.*
New York: Harper & Row, Publishers, Inc., 1950.

Garrison, Webb. *Why You Say It.*
Nashville: Rutledge Hill press, 1992.

Goldsmith, Dolf L. *The Devil's Paintbrush.*
Toronto: Collector Grade Publications, Inc., 1989.

Goldsmith, Dolf L. *The Grand Old Lady of No Man's Land.*
Toronto: Collector Grade Publications, Inc., 1994.

Goodwin, Doris Kearns. *No Ordinary Time.*
New York: Simon & Schuster, 1994.

Hendrickson, Robert. *Encyclopedia of Word & Phrase Origins.*
New York: Facts on File Publications, 1987.

Hunt, Cecil. *Word Origins, the Romance of Language.*
New York: Carol Publishing Group, 1991.

Information Please Almanac.
  New York: Dan Golenpaul Associates, 1975.

Levinson, Leonard. *Wall Street, a Pictorial History.*
  New York: Ziff Davis Publishing Co., 1961.

Manser, Martin. *Get To The Roots.*
  New York: Avon Books, 1992.

Morris, William. *Morris Dictionary of Word and Phrase Origins.*
  New York: Harper & Row Publishers, Inc., 1971.

Rogers, James. *The Dictionary of Cliches.*
  New York: Wings Books, 1985.

The Holy Bible: King James Version.
  Nashville: Thomas Nelson, Inc., 1971.

The Encyclopedia Britannica, 11th edition.
  New York: Simon & Schuster, 1910.

The World Book Encyclopedia.
  Chicago: The Quarrie Corp., 1947.

Webster's New Collegiate Dictionary, 2nd edition.
  Springfield, Mass: G & C Merriam Co., 1958.

Yeoman, R.S. *A guidebook of United States Coins, 25th ed.*
  Racine, Wisc.: Western Publishing Co. Inc., 1971.

Index

A

B

C

D

G

H

I

J

K

L

O

P

Q

R

S

T

Y